A Book of Elements

A Book of Elements

REFLECTIONS ON
MIDDLE-CLASS
DAYS

By Michael Novak

DRAWINGS BY

Karen Laub-Novak

HERDER AND HERDER
New York   St. Louis   San Francisco   Toronto

Acknowledgements

Gratitude is due *The New York Times* for permission to re-print, in altered form, "American Illusion" (April 8, 1971).
But, above all, to Jack Heidenry of Herder and Herder, who first suggested our collaboration, and with good criticism guided us. It has been a good experience: thanks to him.

Herder and Herder
McGraw-Hill Book Company
1221 Avenue of the Americas
New York, New York 10020

123456789 BPBP 798765432

Library of Congress Cataloging in Publication Data

Novak, Michael.
A book of elements.

1. Meditations.   I. Laub-Novak, Karen.   II. Title.
BX2182.2.N68   248'.3   72–3883
ISBN 0–07–073751–7

DESIGNED BY RONALD FARBER

For John and Theodora Cogley

Contents

A Word for Solitude

We conceived this book, poor child, as a way of reflecting together on reliable elements of life. We needed to knit key experiences together.

The emotional demands of our separate crafts are high: hours in studio and study, fears, trepidations, anxieties, enthusiasm, more than a little madness, terror, grief, argument.

Not many artists picture life as we have found it.

Married life, above all, is not what we had been led to expect. Many ignore humble, elementary goods. Not the least of which is petty suffering.

The arts to which we are pledged, moreover, have opposing strengths. The ideal of a lucid prose ignores the thick irrationality which presses outward from the center of our life. Oils and drawings, on the other hand, so far superior in catching the terrors of the soul, are tongueless before the highly verbal audiences of the United States.

Words are a national disease.

Let no one doubt that life together is difficult, and that the conflict between the practical duties of keeping a household going and laboring at our crafts is keen.

We have had to experiment in working together. Sometimes a drawing inspired a verbal reflection; sometimes the reverse. Mostly it was like working in a darkness, groping, trying to find those obscure feelings we knew we wished to render. The writer found it exhausting to remain in the depths achieved by the drawings.

Both drawings and texts spring from a variety of moods, from a number of voices, and from sensibilities in conflict. Harmony is not our suit.

In the texture of daily living, fantasies and fears are as real as sober judgments. Thus the voices and visions recorded here are often imaginary, representing some of the many selves that haunt us.

Our book is meant for browsing, for silence, for leisurely contemplation, for absorption a little at a time. Hours in the sun, in the summer mountains, in the dead of winter, in solitude, are what we had in mind.

We imagine our company proceeding as slowly as we have been forced to do, able to sympathize, to recognize and, perhaps, to cry out in occasional pain.

K. Laub-Novak
Michael Novak

Earth

Begin with Earth and earthy things. What is Earth?
Dot in space and time, spinning, reeling. Begun, perhaps to end. Moment-like. Ethereal perhaps. Fictive,
illusory, net of dreams.

Clinging to the tendrils of a homegrown radish,
soaked in the blood of n hundred millions of our
ill-starred race, holding fast a spinning Moon, be-
witched by Sun: Earth.

2

We make real what we wish to make real. Or perhaps reality is not subject to our wishes?

What I notice and value is real for me. And perhaps what I neglect forces itself on my attention?

What, then, is real?

* * *

Who prepared me for the importance of children in my life? No one. Nothing.

Twenty-two years of school bred virtual ignorance.

Wife and home and stories to the children while work is screaming in my head. Is writing real? Lecturing? Seminars, symposia, colloquia, convocations, conventions, editorial meetings, committees, emergencies?

Ah! but politics. End the war. Build the future. Radic-liberal fight fight

fight

"Tell us a story, dad."

"A scary one!"

"If you get your jammies on."

Music on the air. The night is quiet. Neighbors are asleep. Cold January moonlight in the sky. Long Island Sound is like a silent arm. Below, a sports car briefly tests its wheels against the curve of Bayville Avenue. A city hum is in the village air. The stillness of Iowa unattainable.

I remember the stars in August at Aurora, upper New York State. I had forgotten the sky could be so black. Thousands of stars I had not seen (it seems) since childhood. Walking on the hillside as the grass grew wet. If I lived in upper New York, I would be conservative. Perhaps. To preserve.

On Long Island, the night sky is never black. Mist, light, diffused reflections. And yet I love the human busyness. Pick up the phone and call Manhattan. Friends. Movies, plays, events. Airports. Electricity in the blood.

No one ever told me caring for an old home could be such fun. Three days ago the ice relented, the air grew warmer, so I took a barrel of tar to my third-floor study and crawled out on the roof. Carefully along a gutter to the chimney. Sliver of sidewalk far below. The new brilliant black molasses sheen slippery where a slate had been. Artistry. Patching here, there, a flourish. Lift my gaze. White cirrus across a pale blue sky. If I could climb up over the gable and patch the seam on the other side. White tennis shoes on tiles. It's very steep. More slippery than I anticipate. The tiles give. I slip and begin to fall backwards. Control the tar! Only the chimney catches me.

Continue patching the nearest gable. Back inside. A fleck of tar on the study floor, to recall the day death was merely teasing.

I build a bird feeder, simply.

The snow man the children built sinks like a falling cake. And freezes. Boys next door attack with metal poles. One wide swing and the edge of metal catches Tanya, three, between nose and lip. She screams. The boy knew no interruption of his arc. He is puzzled. She is screaming. Livid white whiplash. Plate broken? Wait and see. Some ice cream, a nap.

Captain Kidd buried chests of treasure between Oyster Bay and Block Island. It could have been in our backyard. "If we find it, daddy, would we be rich?" I didn't realize that Richard, five, knew the meaning of the word.

"Even if we don't find it, you will be Rich."

Tanya's eyes flash. "If . . . if . . . if we find it, would I be Tawn?"

"He'd be Rich and you'd be Tawn."

How well they understand their father's bursts of angry impatience, when he wants to be working but forces himself to help. Acid exasperation. Fixing the tracks for the "hot wheels," for example.

"Why don't you leave?" Richie finally says. "Mommie will help me . . ."

Two

Entirely un-American of me. It's a failing. Every day I welcome the face of Death. Face inside my face.

Pouring through my fingers like sand. Cup my fingers, vainly. Where's it going? so quickly?

During quiet moments every day: surprise. Still alive. Still have time.

Buckling my seat belt in the Plymouth Fury II. Cold. *Click.* Today? Metal, smoke. Glass upon the freeway.

Death is stalking me.

It's positively unpatriotic, in the land of happiness and youth. Morbid perhaps. Neurotic maybe.

Or plain simplicity.

"Granted I must die, how shall I live?"

Speed up the ramp, hurry through the terminal, to the ticket gate barely in time. One hour and forty minutes to Chicago. Memories, memories, of a hundred jet flights to Chicago all become as one.

Death isn't up ahead. It has long since begun.

Death, my love.

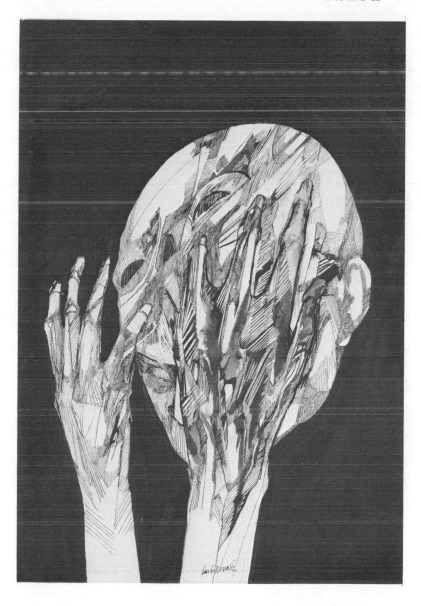

Three

What is time?

Arrow from the past, aiming. "Now" is the tip. How long is "now"? "Now" is never. The moment I am aware of now, now has passed. There is no now. We are constituted out of past and future.

Who am I? A past.

Which past?

Each time I remember it, it is a different past.

No I. No center. No ego. No substance.

It is an April day, unseasonally warm: a bead of sap upon the white rings of the freshly cut maple branch. Viscous. Slowly flowing. Gathers. Hard.

What does it mean to live in time?

I was so sure I had a self, *am* a self, *was* a self. It all seemed plain, certain, common sense.

What is a self? A set of stories. How they shift! Shall I tell you who I am? I cannot do so truthfully. I would cajole, convince, please. I would round it off so that you could *see*. Give it shape. And thus I would embarrass myself, knowing everything is fiction.

There is no category "true biography." There is only "biography now, between me and you." Which is to say invention. Not necessarily lie. Yet surely not "the"

8

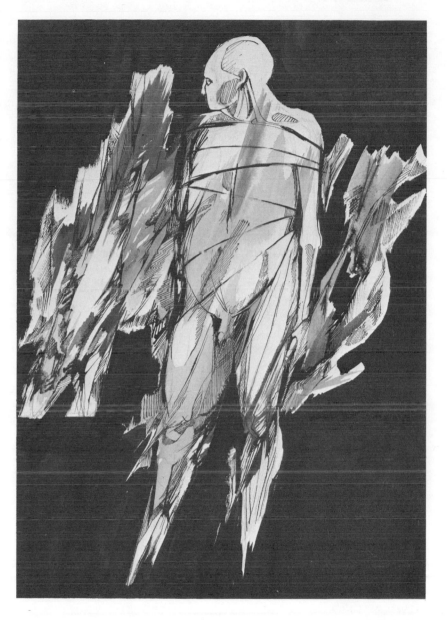

truth. A truth perhaps? Let us say a figment of the truth.

When I am serious, I prove to myself that I do not exist. Above all, in the racy, tangy moments: dive into the clear water on an August day, the pleasure of a perfect *swish* through the basketball net, the stirrings of sexual juices, the moments of perception and community. How exquisite! How sweet! So ripe with forgetfulness.

And then the silence.

Inside is nothing.

It is as true that I do not exist, as that I do exist. Life is very like a dream. I sometimes feel like a spectator, unobtrusive in the dark, unmoved, while a parade of images flickers vividly across a distant stage: my own life, my times, all of it unreal. *What happens* is not the sum of what I am; it is somehow detachable from me. And fantasy can be as real as event.

I do not mean an alienated consciousness. I have never accepted the *cogito* of Descartes. "I think—have a clear and distinct seeing eye, a laser beam of light in the dark—therefore, I am." How absurd! To believe that consciousness is existence. That to be is to be conscious. And to have a problem, then, how consciousness is connected to the body, and whether there is an external world.

The French excel at self-caused alienation, the alienation of mis-imagined consciousness. Thus André Gide in *The Counterfeiters*: "The only existence that anything (including myself) has for me, is poetical . . . It seems to me sometimes that I do not really exist, but that I merely imagine I exist. The thing that I have the greatest difficulty in believing in, is my own reality. I am constantly getting outside myself, and as I watch myself act I cannot understand how a person who acts is the same as the person who is watching him act, and who

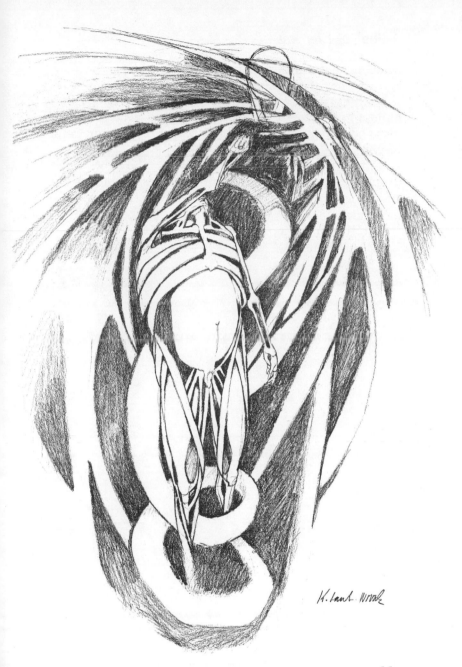

11

wonders in astonishment and doubt how he can be actor and watcher at the same moment."

Nothing is more implausible than modern western philosophy, heroic construction though it be. Nothing more odd, more out of harmony with every instinct and intuition and sense of self.

Better to dance the twist, flickering strobe lights, noise deafening my ears, liquid in my muscles, liquid in the air, liquid everywhere, the sap of life. Wrestling Laocoön, in sweat, tangible to myself as a heavy snake.

I sit, therefore I am.

Seat of wisdom.

Four

CONG HOA SPEAKS:
The moments slide into the sea when I form Chinese
characters. Confucian, Taoist, and Buddhist.

There is the time of daily tasks. I rise. I work. I walk
to the market. Sleep. Love. Watch my children grow,
hair silver, bones begin to stiffen, wisdom accumulate.

There is the time of the heroes. Nothing new under
the sun. A form to let shine through me. Sometimes I
am uplifted. The best my ancestors thought and did
flows like juice through a ripened fruit: I succeed for a
moment in being honest, acting with courage, shrewdly
confounding my enemies, building pride in my sons and
daughters and my villagers.

There is the no-time. When illusions fall like scales:
life is the same. Always the same.

Life is suffering.

It is so sweet.

Life is the pursuit of suffering.

When all illusions fall away and we discover whether
in us lies gold or sandstone, husks or wheat.

Gentleness is a kind of cruelty. Who says that life is
happy tells a great untruth. He lies.

The wisdom of life is to understand its cruelty.
Gently.

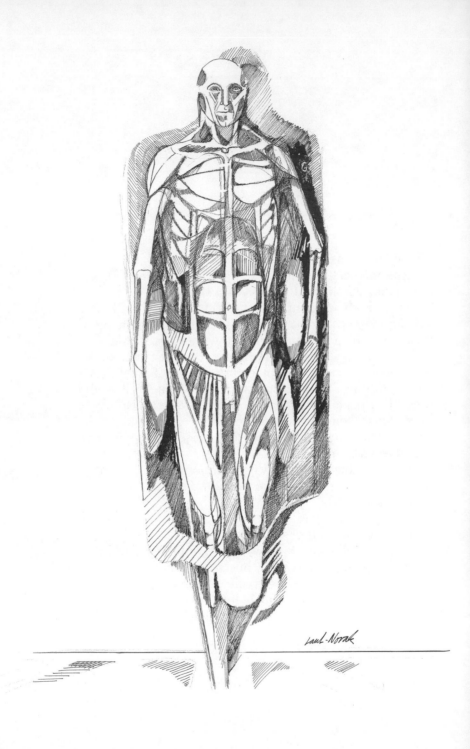

It is an evil existence. One thing alone is good: true recognition. There is no other.

We are made, not for happiness, but for wisdom. The two are contradictory. They never occur together. Only the wise are happy, knowing they are not.

We are made for unhappiness. Unhappiness is all. The only happiness.

And therefore, unutterable peace.

Five

The very notion that life is a parade, a circus, a county fair makes me feel revulsion. For the trouble is that life in America is *not* a parade, a circus, a fair. Imaginatively, our lives are endlessly drab. Kafka: education is a process of killing the imagination. To be modern is to suffocate.

Humans are not products of Reason. We are fruit of Earth. Working with the soil, living with things that bud, bloom, decay. Needing contact with worms, ladybugs, gypsy moths, wrens, dragonflies, mussels, and squirrels as necessarily as we need air. We need to shovel soil, to press seeds with our own fingers into earth, to water, to trim. The basic images of psychic health are learned from Earth. Our ancestors were hunters and farmers. The roots of our own psyches mesh like filaments of a spider with the laws of nature: aggressions and reconciliations.

All night long on television, Reason continues its assault on Earth. Everything natural, organic, and proper to the human body is scorned: "unsightly" hair, "bad" breath, body odors. Nothing, we are told, counts toward acceptability but what has passed through the processes of Reason. The body unaided is ashamed.

Could one imagine a civilization which delighted in the subtle discrimination of kinds of breaths? Early morning breath, coffee break breath, heavy traffic breath,

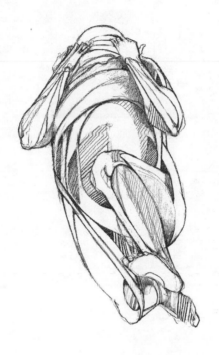

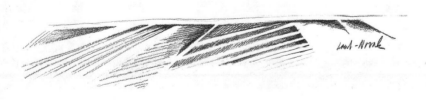

nervous breath, acid stomach breath, smokers' breath, breath after making love, the breath of childhood and of age, of meat eaters and vegetarians, of grease eaters and TV dinner eaters, of athletes and businessmen, of gentle women and shrewish fire eaters? The nose knows more of persons than the eyes. Why do we repress the nose? No scent allowed unless it has been bottled.

Fruit of earth. The body smells. The stomach groans. Farts and burps. Gurgles. Gentle feelings in the stomach and unmentionable storms . . .

Our inner lives are rich. It has become conventional to notice in them only what is practical, reasonable, objective. What deprivation we inflict upon ourselves!

We are reduced to the measurements of the machines among which we spend our lives. Machines require schedules. They impose routines. They are programmed not according to the ebb and flow of our emotions nor to our flights of fancy but to the inflexible processes of Reason. Have ever people sold so much of their inheritance in order to raise their standard of living? Given up so much? So much that was intimate and seemingly inseparable? Given over half their soul?

Machines are good. They demand a price. The price is steep. An Eastern Air Lines pilot landing his 707 at LaGuardia Airport, in ecstasy—it can't be done! An especially interesting sexual life—not a good prospect for most corporations. Has a headache and doesn't come to work—the shiftless, lazy nigger!

In Italy, during a traffic jam, violent arguments and angers and threatened fist fights (no one ever lands a blow): a public rage few Americans allow themselves—fling open the car door, out into the street swinging . . .

Americans sit in their cars and listen to their stomach juices drip.

A meal in Italy often lasts four or five hours, course after course and oh! the conversation. A shave can last longer than an hour—*pat! pat!* In Italy, in order to pray, perhaps humans require "mortification," an asceticism to break the natural rhythms of the earth.

In the United States, please, no more Reason, no "discipline" in the form of rational routine or the deprivation of the senses. Our spirits are too tight. We receive no nourishment from sensuality and fantasy. Our inner lives are starved for sensuousness. (Those ugly restaurants, medieval and feudal and baronial—whose food is processed, without individuality or art).

No, in America our lives are not a parade. They are not a circus. (Remember now those hot, steamy smells —the elephant shit smoking outside the tent doors, the misstep into pungent camel's turd as children crossed

the center ring after the show?) Our very language has been stripped of smells and rough edges: it flows through our lips like brownish water, seldom—what Tanya and Richard call—a *good* grunt. The language too is rationalized, made routine, never abrupt and sharp and threatening. Ever smooth, ingratiating, oil on wheels of the machine. "DO NOT DISTURB!" is evil music for the soul.

Our lives are not a fair. What is a fair? Surprise. The real imagination of real people: amateur but authentic. It *belongs*. Our county fair. Real smells. Unpredictable. "Will those dahlias be good enough to win? Will Teddy [the steer] be big enough by July?" Seeing Teddy through eyes tutored by the sight of other steers his age: learning precise discrimination, in connection with living animals.

A fair is a carnival: fling and foolishness. Jaycees dumped into a barrel of water if you hit the white handle with a ball.

A fair is children's eyes, responding to lights, motion, extravagance. Rides to fear, animals who threaten.

Our lives are not a fair.

Six

I thought, you know, for a long time that I knew where I was going. I loved to work, I really did, *loved* to work, loved hard work, could never do enough, preferred work to play, my play was work. No alienation for me. An income, a touch of fame, and work. A set of plans, loosely held. Libidinal joy: plunging into life, tasting what I could, doing the work I love.

It is so joyous to do only the work one loves! What happiness! For days on end my heart would sing. Rosary beads of blueskied days in California: fifty-nine cloudless days in a row, work going well, joy, pleasure, pride, and lusty life.

Avoidance of too much modern philosophy. Guarding my soul against—shepherding, cupping my hands around a flame—against diseases of consciousness.

How profoundly I hated Sartre, and even Wittgenstein (except that both of them loved flicks, couldn't see enough, never admitted to encountering a bad film). Why did Sartre trap himself inside his own intelligence, and so learn to hate every living thing, nauseous, contemplating self? Wittgenstein's craggy, furrowed, puzzling brow. "Every man over forty is responsible for his own face."

(The mirror shows that I am gaining weight. Soft. No torture there.)

Why do I feel compelled to reflect on this?

Seven

What I love better than any earthly good is liturgy. A
Japanese Noh cycle. Ah! the slow and graceful bows.
Absolute decorum of the body, fluid grace. I would say
control, but it is not controlled. *Sed contra*, the body
flows. The channels are stylized, but there is no control
from the head. The flow originates in the psychic
depths, gushes forth in stunning metaphor.

When is action not an action? When it is measured
by effects.

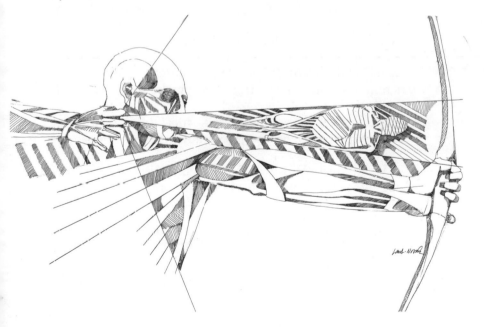

When is action a human action? When it is measured by its inner source.

When is action reasonable? When it does not flow from the head. When it does not manifest control.

There is a saying that romanticism is at war with reason. Ah no! Ah no! That is no war. Children on a seesaw.

To seek the source of human action is to receive the signals of the imagination, the stomach, the sensibilities: to receive them into the intelligence. The intelligence? Ah, I did not say into analysis or words.

What is best in intelligence cannot be said. What is best in intelligence is not analysis.

What is best in intelligence is not passion, emotion, sensitivity, sensibility, the stomach, intuition, the imagination, perception . . .

Why, in fact, am I singling out "intelligence"?

Because I am not a romantic. Nor a rationalist.

What is best in intelligence is "hitting the mark." Absorbing everything, profiting by everything, devouring nothing, making a slave of nothing, manipulating nothing.

What is best in intelligence is "hitting the mark."

Intelligence is not "a thing." There is not some *thing* in me to be identified as "intelligence." Intelligence is a response called forth from me by the abyss in which I swim.

Intelligence is world-and-self, me, suffused with at least a partial light, in joy. Intelligence is an act of world-and-me.

What am I? World and self fecundating one another, not adequately separable from one another: world-in-self and self-in-world. We are, to the world, like a foetus in a womb. (One day, the world will abort us.)

What am I? This fluid, slippery, elusive, objectless, unfathomable, never still, always hiding "I"? I am that which I am most ignorant of.

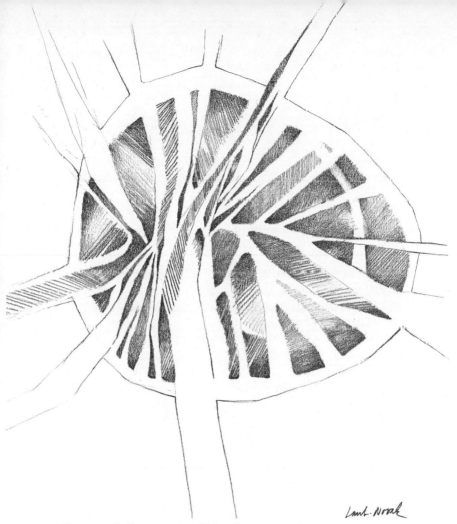

Frank Novak

Time and I—most solid of assumptions, most personal, most indubitable—of them do I know least among all matters to be known. (Of only one other matter is my ignorance more vast: of God.)

Time, I, God: in a seaswirl. Vertiginous.

Of one thing I am sure: I am conscious and my body is alive. Yet "I" do not exist, except as world. The more I inquire, the more the sands give way.

Who—what—am I?

A question put to mother earth, perhaps.

Eight

The Words of Cong Hoa:
It is, after all, a dream.

Politics is an illusion.

History is an illusion.

There is only nature. Nature and the self. Envelope and letter, shell and nutmeat, body and blood.

Ever the same.

Is the sin of the West intelligence? Not the intelligence of wisdom. Rather, the intelligence of power.

The sin of the West is history. Where Judaism erred: in imagining that a messiah will come, that there is a hope in the light of which the prophet may lash the abuses of the present. Where Christianity erred: it banked everything upon the future.

The future is not different from the past.

In the caves men practiced the highest arts. They loved. They raised their children. They endured. They survived.

"Primitive" humans did not love their neighbors less, nor murder more of their neighbors, nor yield to fear, bitterness, and frustration more than modern humans.

The pursuit of utopia is the primal madness of the race. It is, if one may humbly say so, the original sin. The pursuit of "if only," the pursuit of a better world through chemistry, the pursuit of the kingdom of God upon the earth.

Do you value God? Have reverence for him? Do not bring him into the world of illusions, where he cannot live, breathe, or have his being, where he must of necessity suffocate and die.

Who brings God into history kills God.

Nine

I love to write. It is perhaps my keenest joy—most truly me. When I try to take a vacation, I grow restless. Not from guilt. Not from compulsion. From a dark complex of motives I cannot disentangle: a delight in writing, a driving ambition, a dread that the brief years are slipping, like air through my fingers—all will be over soon, and so little of my life's work has been done.

"When you are depressed, or low," a canny friend mentioned, "I notice that you write another article."

Art and neurosis. Why *do* I write? What demons impel me? What rages like translucent coals burn within?

What difference would it make to isolate the exact impelling force? The point is to channel that welling energy as best I can, with all the freedom, joy, and gentle care at my disposal: clutching sand in my fingers, not willingly to lose a grain.

In another sense, there is no art apart from the demons in oneself. To write is to wrestle with tormentors. It is to meet the enemy. Ambitions and vanities, dreads I cannot bring to tongue, fears, angers, joys, and ecstasies. Often I am so full of joy I cannot fathom it. Yet far below, a vein whence every word I have written springs: a troubled, peaceful vein. When inner quiet descends as deep as that there is a music in my life. I listen to a tune. It races far ahead of my pen, I chase

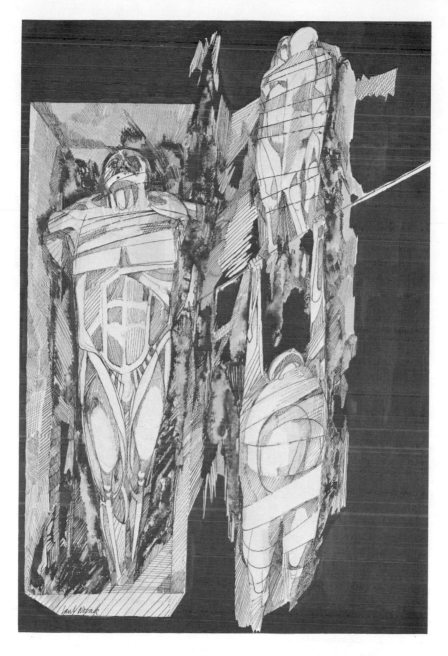

29

it, stumbling on brambles, falling into sinkholes, bruising my spirit as I race after it. The soul is so quiet, so still, the pen refuses to record it. I see the failure and am pained.

I would rather wrestle with that pain than any other good in life. Such combat is the source of all that is best in me, of everything I value: whatever of honesty, whatever of that self-knowledge which is ignorance, whatever the depth of judgment, whatever the sensitivity to inward nuance in myself or in others.

On the Last Day, when the Lord says: "Stand forth. Be illumined!", all else in me will burn away, but that shall stand. Fierce little light, which is not mine. No idol is it. It is not in my control. It changes, grows, embarrasses itself. Before it I feel awe. I worship. It is that in me which is not me: closer to me than I to myself, no alien, no magic, no other. But a participation in another: me and not-me, my truth but not possessed by me, truth shattering, truth expanding, truth quieting, my life but more than my life.

Writing is my prayer. It is my contemplation. It is my love.

Ten

Is it enough to believe in God? Is it enough to celebrate the Eucharist with friends? I am not responsible
for history. What my government does, it does in my
name, yes, but that is a legal fiction. Who am I to
criticize those with primary responsibility and better information?

Can a person be a Christian without being politically
alert? Suppose my understanding, and my votes, and my
actions are building up the Kingdom of God on earth:
Kingdom of Justice, Truth, Love, Liberty. My prayers,
then, are in tune with my actions.

Otherwise, my prayers would say "we" . . . "*Our
Father*" while my actions would be divisive.

The difference between nineteenth-century piety and
twentieth-century piety seems to lie in political consciousness. Every political act has theological conse-
quences. Every theological utterance can be contradicted
by political action, or inaction.

Adolf Hitler proved the point. Those Christians who
believed that religion is separate from politics, and
church from state; those Christians who believed that
the sphere of religion lies in the private consciousness
of the individual; those Christians who believed that
the highest Christian value is obedience, good order, and
the safety of national unity—those Christians *obeyed*.

They marched in Hitler's armies. They served. They ignored the existence of the gas ovens, the death camps, the gray smoke of burning human flesh from the crematoria. They stood up for God and country, and they marched.

What have we learned from the Hitler period?

That obedience is no excuse. God will not, on the Last Day, accept the plaint: "But I was only following orders."

His reply is likely to be (if we may dare guess the inscrutable): "Why did I put a head on your shoulders? Were you not responsible and free?"

"Oh, but it would have meant jail and torture, and my family . . ."

"Crucifixion?"

My cheeks burn.

And shall we show the world that not only Germans, but also citizens of the United States are quiet in the face of war crimes? Shall we show the world how loyal we were, how eagerly we obeyed, how gentle and polite we were in never once disrupting public order while five million fellow human beings were forcibly driven from their homes? While bombs and artillery fell freely upon "free-fire" zones? More bombs, three times more bombs, than the allies dropped upon all of Europe and all of the Pacific theater in World War II?

Imagine living with one's children as a peasant in Vietnam. Imagine large, well-armed soldiers moving freely across one's land, into one's home, giving orders in a strange language, doing what they felt they had to do . . . losing the members of one's family one by one, losing one's home, one's livelihood . . .

And what shall we learn after the war? Will we be increasingly horrified as the facts come out? What shall we tell our children? How shall we look our grandchildren in the eye?

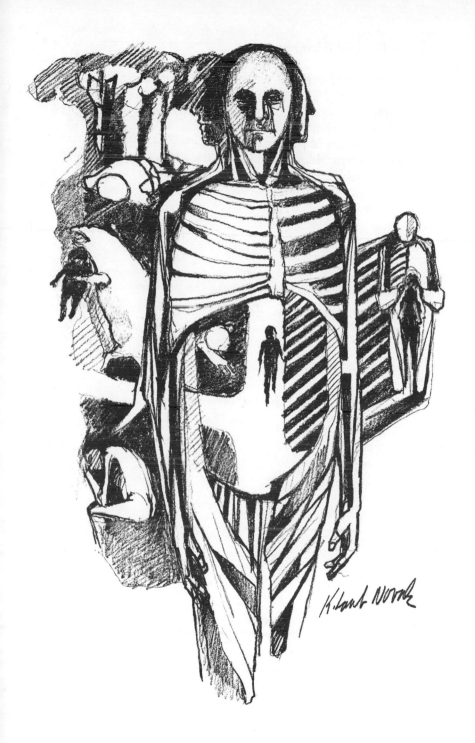

It is not easy to celebrate the Eucharist while the screams of diving planes are in one's ears, before one's eyes the craters of the moon where a village used to be . . . grandmother with an American's M-16 at her temple, grandchild's brains spilled out across the earth . . . rice growing blood-red, nets of napalm crackling across the trees.

"A better world through chemistry."

We know not what we do.

Eleven

I have loved so many things in life. It isn't fair to live but once!

Red, blue, green: brightly colored jackets of the *Summa Theologica.* Thirty shiny volumes, hefty and hard. How many happy hours I have spent wandering through Latin pages! How marvelous it would be again, to sit with six or seven students who read it furiously and eagerly. A peace is hidden there, earthy wisdom . . . Sadness now, foreseeing neither time, nor occasion, nor a group of students at peace enough to allow me to return before I die to books like those . . .

I recall a simple thought of his. *So unified are body and soul that a sign of their unity is as follows: a warm bath and a good dinner recreate the spirit.* May I recall as well his lines on the realism and yet the ecstasy of love?—lucidly explored, lucidly linked. And on the relations of the passions to intelligence? On the effects of acquired habits (a "life style") on the judgment?

My love for Aquinas is so deep I believe nothing will uproot it—a love not exactly for the sentences on the pages which he left (though an interpreter finds much to marvel at in those) but for the living intelligence, the calm, the sweetness of the man.

When the enlightened man today opens Aquinas it is to three texts chiefly (witness the anthologies upon my shelves) that he turns: on hell, on the burning of heretics, and on law. Whereas he *might* have chosen lovely passages on wisdom, joy, love, trust, mercy, intelligence, judgment, the simplicity of God . . . A century hence, men will wonder how the enlightened tolerated assembly lines, the brutalization of the urban poor, and napalm.

It is a weakness of mine, perhaps, to take the evil, blindness, and harshness of men for granted, and to marvel at marks of beauty and grace occasionally achieved. We begin in savagery, and never break completely free.

A single act of wisdom, of generosity, of grace—surprising, uncalled for, free, victorious.

Twelve

Drabness drags us down. A sea of yellow slime. The colorless gas: routine, pettiness, days that pass into days.

Making those alive is art. Eschewing the "new," being suspicious of the merely "exciting," building up creative things the way a forest grows: silently, without appearing to move at all. A thousand days of sunlight, scores of days of rain, to make a tiny shoot of evergreen grow strong enough to stretch.

Wisdom does not lie in the pursuit of distraction. Freedom does not consist in seeking excitement. Novelty is almost always superficial.

One conquers dullness not by moving one's body but by changing one's soul. The quality of perception, and feeling, and sympathy is not injured by circumstance. Once one has attained enough identity and integrity to stand alone, one can grow in any circumstance: in solitude, in prison, in exile, in confused and dreary and desolate surroundings. Soul triumphs.

* * *

There is a difference between poverty and brutalization. In poverty (among the world's poor in some places), the soul is intact, and grows in wisdom and in strength.

Jesus lived in an "underdeveloped country" at a very

early stage in the "march of progress." Were people around him insensitive or stupid? Or primitive? Or savage?

And those around the Buddha? Or in thirteenth-century Japan?

Brutalization, however, deprives a man of his identity. It is not so much a matter of pride or dignity. A person lacks a future; he lacks esteem; he sees himself in the eyes of others as a thing, loathed, contemned, arousing faint and yet distinct fears. The "look" he gets from others devastates him. He is a nothing. He does not exist. They are afraid, they hurry away, they speedily forget.

He is not a human being. Three-fifths of a human being, to be exact.

Thirteen

THE THOUGHTS OF CONG HOA:
Mostly we are clay. Mostly we are not awake. Mostly
we scavenge, like the alley cat: dejected, without community, dependent on events.

They say that Americans are activist. You ask my
modest observation? Americans are puppies. How much
affection they daily need! A people in search of reas-
surance.

What you call "progress" is more primitive than the
hill tribes of the Anshan Valley. There, at least, men
belong to one another. Each is known. Each is loved.

Men's need for one another is the greatest need of
all.

There is only one progress: a deeper, truer, more solid
feeling of community.

I do not mean the suspicion of fellow villagers, curi-
ous to know everything about each: that Xuan has
taken a mistress, or that Thai scolds her children.

I do not mean the marching of young men and the
shouting of slogans against imperialists.

I do not mean the "brotherhood" of lodges of Rotar-
ians. (Oh yes, I have been asked to "talk" at Rotarian
dinners.)

I mean the sense of belonging, of man to man: the
desire to be conscious of life and its necessities. The un-

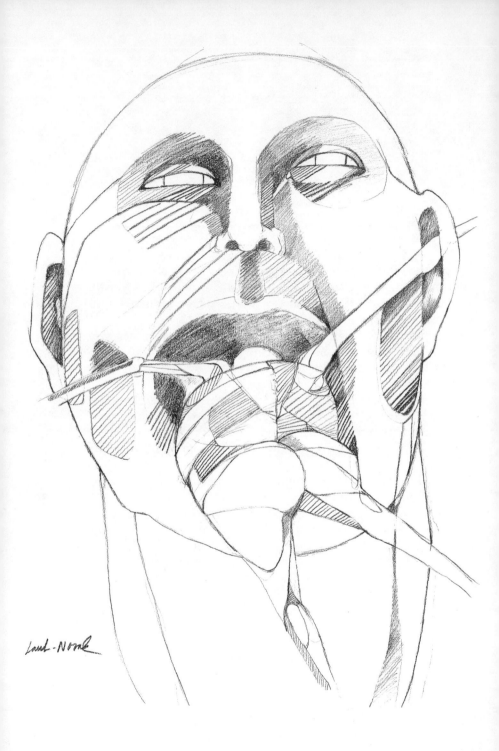

willingness to cause hurt. Support through praise, gentleness, and honor.

The ego is an early violet. March frost shrivels it.

If you injure an ego, what is left to man?

The most progressive world is a world in which every single human has value. *His* value. In the eyes, in the words, in the actions of others.

Act always so as to confer value. Let your eyes say to every other: "You are of value to me and in yourself. You do not need my eyes to tell you that."

Appreciation is the highest ethic, the most progressive life.

The competitive life, the "meritocratic" life—what are its fruits? Many beautiful and powerful *things.* Huge *machines.* And deflated humans.

Appreciation. A social order built on any other rock is primitive.

Is it true that Americans are the only people in the world who humiliate their infants and their children in public? I have watched them in Howard Johnson's, along the highways: the scolding and the public fury.

A more savage practice is unknown to me.

Fourteen

We watch our parents growing old. Their lives are hard. Their children did not become what they dreamed of.

Their dreams were simple dreams. Families were close. Each able person worked. The world was intact. Within that world, one knew what to do. Some performed more perfectly than others. Their children would, gently, be the best.

Their world exploded. Children scattered to the winds. Values have changed, standards, practices. Scarcely anything about their children's lives is "right." And does "right" change? Not easily for them.

The suffering of spirit is intense.

Age, too. When memory slips. Aren't fathers supposed to know everything? Then why does my father now seem helpless, needing to be cared for? And sometimes so unhappy?

Why are the old lonely? Why do their hearts hurt?

Why don't their emotions atrophy?

"When you be dead," Richie comforts me, "I will bury you. I will not be dead, will I?"

"No, not then, Richie. But when you grow old."

The first television politician he recognized, when he was two, was Bobby Kennedy, during the California campaign of 1968. By accident, he saw the shooting repeated on the evening news.

It was hard to explain to him: "Dead." And "why."

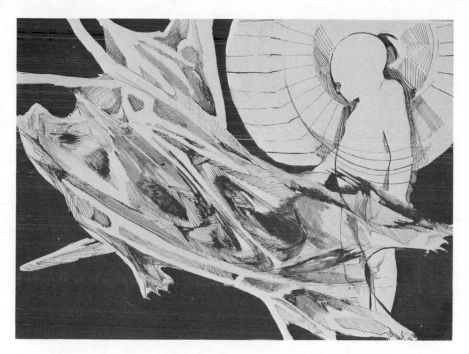

The next November, walking near our home among noisy autumn leaves, he found a dead chipmunk, flattened, stiff, almost dust.

"What's that?"

"It's dead."

That word came back to him a second time. "Like Bobby Kennedy?"

Yes.

Watching parents grow old, one finds one's thoughts growing old. Unspoken loves, loyalties, resentments, complexities. Many find it hard to visit parents. This is especially true among immigrant peoples, where there are differences in education. At a distance, warm gulf-stream emotions. Close up, a deep bitter anger flares. A need to hurt. A dry, distant, cold abstractedness. A chill defense.

How can parents and children know so little about

one another? Can the emotions of each ever be untangled? And if untangled, spoken?

Our parents, I fear, shall go into the grave without ever hearing vague, inarticulate emotions which sometimes choke us, a complexity we cannot fathom, a trail we cannot uncover.

Superficially, we hold so many things *against* them. Not real, but symbolic things. Why don't they *see* what we have chosen, the route that we are following?

Human cultures are so many, so diverse, that when we enter one we lose contact with those in another. America is such that it makes strangers of us all. "Upward mobility," centrifugal of soul.

Why are we not strong enough to cut a light through our emotions, and make connections? Not the culture out there, but we ourselves: there the burden rests.

If we cannot be limpid with our parents, then what hope is there for the unity of our race?

And yet . . . and yet . . . life, it seems is fundamentally alone. Down the years, parents and children who have been close, whose emotions are strong and strongly shown, seek fruitlessly the paths of articulation. Poor gestures must suffice. Squeezes of the hand.

Death, death. One approaches it alone. Fierce darkness. Demons. A thicket of joy, regret, and hope recedes: eyes riveted upon the empty stairs whence footfalls already rise. Not, of course, consciously. Consciously, life seems more full than ever. Hidden far from sight the eye of truth glares out.

Footfalls.

Mother! Dad!

Fire

Which all nature is, a Heraclitean fire: mud that
stiffens, cakes, is swept by wind, erodes, and shifts;
leaves that yellow, redden, spangle, twist, release,
blow and rot, to push up jonquils near the wall . . .
Passion and war, love and leaping hatred, vio-
lence and dedication. Build and burn.
Shifting as the shadows of a giant cloud upon the
waving wheat.

Fifteen

A passage that says more than any instincts of my stomach. Speechless, I read:

[*Congressional Record*, March 1, 1971. Testimony of former U.S. Servicemen.]

STEVE NOETZEL: At Can Tho they had a python snake, which is a constrictor . . . many times when they brought prisoners in and were going to interrogate them the next day, they put them in a room, dark room, with the python snake and let them struggle with that thing all night . . . We could hear them screaming in there almost all night.

MIKE MCCUSKER: Every dead Vietnamese was counted as Viet Cong, because they would not be dead if they were not Viet Cong, whether they were 90 years old or six months old. The body count was any pool of blood, and I used to think that perhaps multiplied by seven . . . And perhaps that was the most degrading atrocity; the garbage cans of the different battalions and companies, they would allow one or two Vietnamese to empty these garbage cans into their buckets—which also let the Marines think, after these farmers were reduced to nothing else, that these people must be inferior if they lived out of garbage cans . . .

DANIEL K. AMIGONE: On the ranges when you are firing . . . you're taught by your instructor to holler "kill"

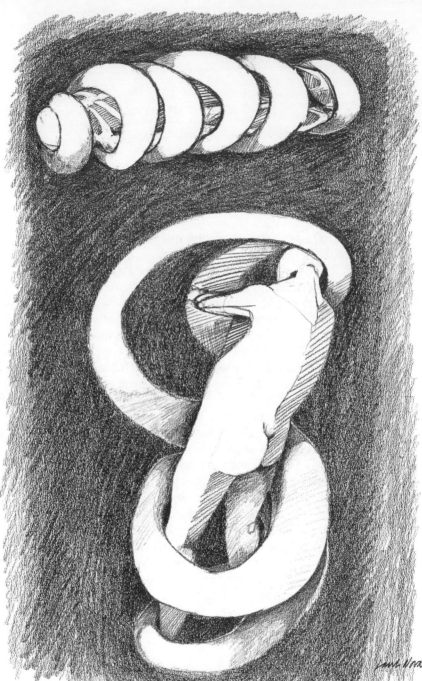

every time you squeeze that trigger, and you're killing a gook, as they call them . . .

PHILIP WINGENBACH: While we were going through the city, people were celebrating . . . We were leaving the outskirts . . . and our second man in the second jeep opened up on the village with a 50-cal. machine gun. As soon as he started firing, everyone else started firing . . . We opened up on them for about 20, 30 seconds as we rode by . . . There were people coming out of the hootches, screaming, crying, "No VC, no VC, we're not Vietcong." We went up to them and there were people lying inside the first four hootches in the village. Dead children, women, men—we didn't count— we didn't even stick around, because we knew what would happen. Guys in my unit just wanted to kill people . . . They don't care who they kill, as long as they're Vietnamese, or gooks, as we called them . . . The chief of the village made a complaint . . . There were no weapons found in the village at all . . . In the morning, before everyone went in [to the battalion commander's inquiry], the platoon sergeant had said, "You guys just remember the right story," and that was it, and it was understood.

GREG MOTOKA: The lieutenant's orders were very specific to the machine gunner and to me to shoot anybody that comes down that trail. Anybody. He made no specifications or qualifications whether they were carrying weapons or not. Well, someone came down the trail. It was a woman carrying her child. And following our lieutenant's orders, they were shot. And the only thing the lieutenant had to say about that was, "Let's get out of here."

PETER NORMAN MARTINSEN: I found the man's hands had been tied to an Army field table . . . and the lieutenant was placing bamboo splinters under the man's fingernails. At the same time the Specialist 6 was "ring-

ing him up" (administering electrical shocks) around
his ears with a field telephone. Later on, the lieutenant
was reprimanded very badly for leaving marks on the
man, because the credo of intelligence work and POW
interrogation is, you do not leave marks. Do anything
you want, but do not leave marks. In other words, cover
yourself.

KENNETH BARTON OSBORN: A detainee, not a POW, but
a detainee, was put in another cage, and he was forced
to lay on the floor with his hands tied behind his back
and they would insert . . . a wooden peg, a dowel with
a sharpened end, into the semicircular canal of the ear,
which would be be forced into the head little by little
as he was interrogated. And, eventually, it did enter the
brain and killed the subject, the detainee. They never
got any viable information out of him—they called that
a loss but in any case there was one thing that was a
standard operating procedure. And I asked the lieutenant, I said, how often do you do this kind of thing? He
said, whenever we can't get information by easier methods . . . If they wanted to interrogate detainee A, they
would take someone along who was either in bad health
or whom they had already written off as a loss—take
both these Vietnamese along in the helicopter and they
would start investigating detainee B, the one they had
no interest in, and they couldn't get any information
out of him and so they would threaten to throw him
out of the helicopter. All the time, of course, the detainee they wanted information from was watching. And
they would threaten and threaten and, finally, they
would throw him out of the helicopter. I was there
when this happened twice and it was very effective, because, of course, at the time the Step One was to throw
the person out of the helicopter and Step Two was to
say, "You're next." That quite often broke them down.

GORDON LIVINGSTON: The standing order of the regiment was to "find the bastards and pile on." That was printed on signs in every bivouac area. And that, in fact, is what the chaplain prayed for when asked to pray for a large body count. He said, "Help us, Oh Lord, to fulfill the standing order of this regiment. Give us the wisdom to find the bastards, and the strength to pile on . . ."

Sixteen

The Catholic people carry with them stories and symbols which suggest the cruelty and irrationality of life, the corruptibility of men, the brutality of power. Yet Catholic theology has a reputation for rationality and legalism.

Sociology is not the same as theology. A group stresses theologically what socially and personally it is most deficient in. The law of compensation.

A Protestant stresses "justification by faith" and minimizes "works." But nothing is easier than to play upon a Protestant's guilt. How he longs to be perfect, reasonable, enlightened, "fully human"! How hard he works at it!

Jews write about alienation. Yet family ties are thick and familial, emotions dense. The encouragement given each child to be the best, the very best, must be seen to be believed. "Nothing is too good for little Allan . . ." Secretary of State, at least.

A Harvard professor: "Protestants tend toward insanity; Catholics toward corruption; Jews toward self-pity; atheists toward suicide."

Descended from a long line of Renaissance popes! Our ancestors did not fear power or its uses. Tough, cynical, cruel. The early popes rushed into a power vacuum in Europe, and did not scruple to fill it until better men rose up to take the power from them.

See at the Mass what happened to God's son. Political execution, after a political trial: "Expedient for the nation." To calm the flood of revolutionary movements, a living eagle spiked to the door. His dark red blood shed by imperial command.

Jesus is the Word interpreting our lives: Darkness cannot tolerate the good. Life is not reasonable. Life belongs, not to Enlightenment, but to the Father of Lies.

So we descend from medieval popes. Let it not be said Catholics are afraid of dirty hands.

Call power, power; irrationality, irrationality; interests, interests. The point of running in elections is to win. But not worth losing one's soul for.

Should we prefer that politics be a matter of *communication* (new sacrament of the Word)? . . . participation, committee meetings, discussion, discussion, discussion, and consensus? Ah! if politics could be more rational, requiring nothing more violent than pressure laid upon the air by lips expressing words. (A hen's ass.) Have an *open meeting*, ask *questions*, come to an *understanding*. A genteel vote.

Faith in reason: proportional to one's height in the establishment.

Because theology is acquiring, as it must, political consciousness, many religious people are leaving the churches. The churches are "irrelevant." What is "real" is radical politics.

Ironic: finding church politics too messy, too slow, too difficult, many turn to city hall.

Yes, every theological judgment has political implications. Every political action, or inaction, expresses a theological commitment. It does not follow that religion is politics, or politics religion.

A theology brought to political consciousness remains theology.

To say "politics" is to say "human." It is also to say

55

"realm of illusion," "absurd," "evanescent," "insubstantial."

Politics is not salvation, not enlightenment, not purification. It requires a wisdom of its own, which must be tempered to the crowd, the majority, a low common denominator. It offers, on the human ship, the sweaty laboriousness of the boiler room.

Applaud the boilermakers.

Seventeen

CONG HOA SPEAKS:
The world is one and all the good things of the world
are one. In America, you prefer the many. You see everything discrete. Believe me, all wisdom is not confined
in the Orient.

Wisdom is one as the world is one.

Can it be possible that from one Source mutually
incompatible ways arise? The power that through the
blue sky drives the Phantom jet, through the rice drives
nourishment.

Dream, illusion, and reality blend. What in America
is called "reality" is, as well, illusion.

Mystics of mathematics, inebriate of the new.

Children do not know what to do with their shiny
toys. They set them aside and look for others.

You are underdeveloped now. You will learn.

We do not hate you, you understand. Despite what
you have done to our country, our villages, our families.
I speak no less than truth. My intention is not to raise
feelings of guilt in you.

On the contrary. I have the impression that you are
too easily moved by guilt. That guilt is the emotion
which dominates your lives.

I listen, do you understand, to your orators and states-
men and journalists. Even to professors. The most fa-

mous among you win notice by making the others guilty. Every day I learn about a new "crisis." A new "neglect." A new "concern."

If a man went to sleep for a year, and then asked, he would not know what the most recent guilt might be. He would not know which words he should no longer say. Or which words are "in."

You are an easily dominated people. It is quite easy to tyrannize you. As a Vietnamese, I am accorded every honor. No one dares to contradict me. Ignore me, yes, for I am not one of you, I do not really count. I am not American and hence am only "interesting." I do not—cannot—"really" understand. For reality belongs to America, the cutting edge of progress. Who among you would wish to be anything but progressive?

That is the form of guilt that most interests me. Americans are the only people I have met—in Asia, in Europe—who, when they ask you, "What do you think of our country?", are really nervous that you might not like it. They are the only ones so easily influenced by what others think.

There is something very winning about this. My wife and I often speak of it. Will you forgive me? Americans are so like children. We talk to them as we talked to our youngsters, before they left us.

You need encouragement. You need affection. You try to be too many things. You do not know what you wish to be. You have not known defeat. You have never, as a people, been broken on the rack of life. You don't know if you could endure it. That is why you are afraid. You are not certain that you can endure it. That is why you are afraid. You are not certain that you can endure.

Electronics and computers cannot buy you that security. We have a teaching in the East. It is this: If you wish to be secure, you must enter insecurity.

St. John of the Cross is at one with Taoism here.

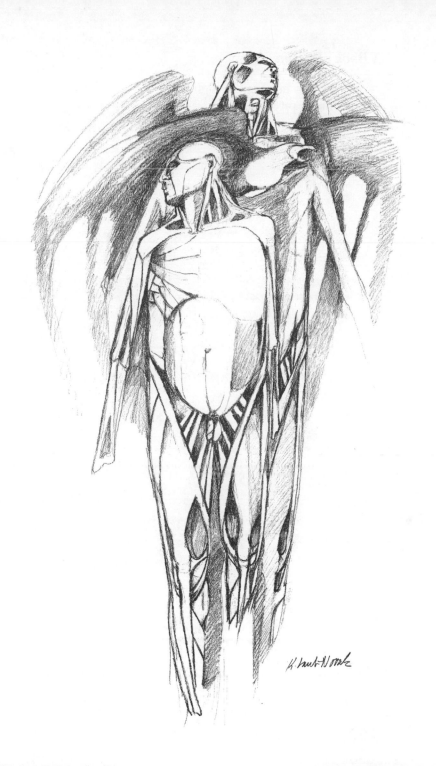

America has not known night.
For this we pity you.
You will.
For all our sakes.

Eighteen

Remember when sentences used to describe—me!—as an "angry young man"?

Away for three days, my wife telephones: "How have the children been?"

"Fine. Except I've lost my voice. From yelling."

"Oh no!"

Yes. Why do I get so angry, about trivial things? An associate delays me with an error, and the rage that breaks from me then, oh, my chevalier!

It is not the anger itself that disturbs me. I like people who get angry. I like the anger in myself. Have you ever heard a man praised: "I like the fact that you are engaged. You are not detached."

It is not anger that disturbs me. Aquinas: "Only those who love grow angry." Indifference does not lead to anger.

Anger springs from love, rage from repression, resentment from self-depreciation. It is the rage and the resentment in myself that trouble me. There are so many things I hate. Their root lies in a certain hatred of myself.

Why do I hate myself? I wish I knew.

Love of self is harder, even, than love of neighbor. I don't mean conceit, arrogance, complacence, self-preoccupation. Why would those arise, except that we do not love ourselves, cannot be honest, direct, and natural?

Love of self is the first and greatest gift of all. A look into a pool, not to see one's own visage, but deep within, limpidly, peacefully, a view of what God sees in me, intends in me: no more, no less.

How wonderful it would be to love myself! I wish I could.

Restless, restless, restless. Not the itch to grow, not the dynamic of development . . . sheer self-hatred . . . the need to move, escape, and find some ecstasy.

"God save me from a woman who does not love herself."

God save me from me.

A bright young shining boy, round-faced, idolized, hair perfectly in place, certain that he is a god. No, not *such* self-love. Not the reflection of a mother's love.

Not even a tranquil conscience.

A sense of truth, restfulness, no need to justify or to be justified: content to stand in the gaze of God, erect, upright, unbroken by my sins against the Light, pretending neither to goodness nor to evil, content even not to be of interest: simply me. I, Lord. Substance of your intention. Posited against the nothingness, a calibrated weight, precisely known.

(Bag of beans tossed in one's hand, set down.) Being.

Luther saw the world as a bar of judgment. None could stand before the scouring Judge. "Sinner: Fall down."

Wilhelm Reich, penis in the air, calls himself divine. "I am god."

Neither contrite, nor godlike.

But simply: "I am."

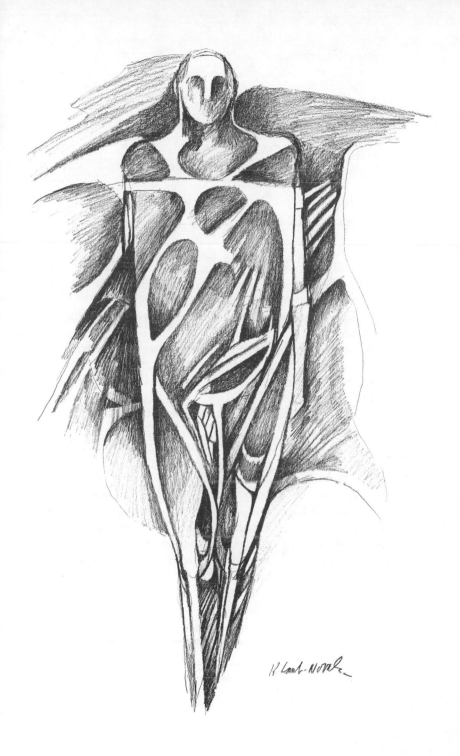

Nineteen

Is repression in sexual matters damaging? The modern and liberated person, it seems, does what he wants when he wants, with consenting adults.

I have sometimes worried that I am not sufficiently liberated.

So many notions I once held I no longer hold. So often in the past my views have been subject to change. Perhaps here, too.

Life speeds swiftly by. A mistake may be irretrievable: Imagine concluding at fifty-five that chastity had been an error.

Thus it happened that I attached a great deal of importance to sexual liberation.

Henry Miller, D. H. Lawrence, Norman Mailer, Hemingway, Joyce—nearly every modern author—placed pressure upon my soul. I felt it as pressure. Notions of chastity, virginity, fidelity, and restraint, in which I had been nourished, seemed conventional and not altogether soundly based. The Christian tradition is so negative and so unreliable on sexual matters that it is difficult to put one's trust in it. How can one take St. Augustine seriously on sexual ethics?

A man, modern authors seem to say, must demonstrate virility. Women may *say* one thing; in fact, they want to be mastered.

64

Imperatives of virility, imperatives of gentleness. They are not contradictory, of course. The great lovers of history reputedly practiced both. (Empirical confirmation comes mostly through their diaries.)

What to do?

It was a conflict.

Lo and behold! Women's liberation. Women do not want to be treated as things, objects. Kate Millett doesn't *like* Norman Mailer and D. H. Lawrence and Henry Miller.

One doesn't *have* to imitate the sexual giants. Sexual liberation is not the life of the hunter or the hunted.

It's much more civilized. Equal partners equally consent, after conversation, when they want to. No manipulation, no oppression.

Thank God for women's liberation! It has restored an ethic of persons. Taken seriously, it may restore standards of chastity *Playboy* never dreamed of.

Then, of course, comes "J," *The Sensuous Woman*. Back to Henry Miller!

Why on earth is sexual aberration—wildest fantasy—so attractive? And why does an uninhibited generation end in nothingness, alienation, and the celebration of disgust? *Play It As It Lays* . . .

Couldn't one just compromise, with a little bit of infidelity, a little bit of wildness? Steady infidelity seems to bore. Just a little bit?

The possibility of danger enlivens life. Flirtation is better than reality. That was ever the strength of ritual, taboo, and chastity.

Twenty

How many centuries has it been since a serious writer wrote in favor of authority? The word to which we flock is freedom. The "authoritarian personality" is fascist. Vince Lombardi, for example, was a fascist. Military men are fascist.

One of the great conflicts in American life: between football coaches and intellectuals.

I dreamed the other night of a perfect world. No one made demands on anybody else. Society asked nothing of individuals. Each person expressed libidinal energies frankly, fearlessly, and freely. Everyone displayed courage and honesty. Breakthroughs occurred every day.

No one was troubled by feelings of guilt. Inhibitions were ice cubes in August: silver remnants in the gin.

Then I had a nightmare, and awoke in a fever. My brow was sweating. My pajama pants were wet. When my heart ceased its rapid breathing, I recovered the rough outlines of what had so grievously disturbed me.

Remove emperors, church authority, the divine right of kings, and patriarchal Freudian fathers. Does that mean that authority is done with? Invent democracy, and arrange its practices so that small communities participate in "decisions that affect their lives." Does that mean that authority has been banished? I began to scream . . .

Authority is variable: it changes colors, shapes, meth-

66

ods, and appearances. In one circumstance, officialdom is favored; in another, the boldest personality—the one with the most forthright ego, strongest sense of immediate direction, most touching complaint, loudest mouth.

What is absolutely noticeable about human beings: their need for authority. It is not a weakness. It is part of what it is to be human.

Authority is necessary because we are finite. We can go forward in n directions. But neither our resources nor the time at our disposal is infinite. Insofar as we wish to set a clear direction, be decisive, establish priorities, we must choose. Some one, some group, some procedure must be empowered, or there is no choice. Without choice, there is no freedom. Authority is an expression of freedom.

Authority is not the contradictory of freedom but its precondition.

No one, meanwhile, can think of everything at once. Most of the time, I don't want to be bothered with the boiler room. Let some one else work out the details, attend the committee meetings, make the hard decisions. I want as much time free for the things I love as I can shelter. For this reason, too, authority is a precondition of freedom.

It was a tragic mistake when in the mythmaking of modern history men opposed "freedom" to "authority," and imagined these two to be at war.

There are many men of liberal principles whose manner is authoritarian and manipulative. Many men of conservative principles act in a liberating and enabling way. Beware of ideology. Look to the man.

The early heroes of liberal enterprise—the scientists, experts, pragmatists, and engineers of a rational society —are they not the new authorities, with their democratic and enlightened principles and their rituals of the reasonable?

Authority is indispensable on a finite planet, of finite

resources, and infinite aspiration. (Practicing "live and let live," letting the strongest survive, perhaps we could do with very little authority—just enough to flex the muscles of the strong against the weak. Businessmen and scientists might wrestle for pre-eminence; or inter-marry.)

Let us assume that authority is indispensable. And keep a sharp eye upon its changing shapes. We need authority, in order to be free.

Freedom is the master, authority the servant: good and necessary servant, all the same.

Twenty-One

THE SPEAKER IS CONG HOA:

I am often struck by the goodness of the people of America. Not in the way that Richard Nixon says that they are good: "America is a good nation." No, he means something altogether different—and erroneous.

Americans are simple, like peasants in many countries, yet less parochial. They know more about the world. They sympathize on a universal scale.

A Vietnamese was talking in a tavern with some truck drivers. He asked them if they'd heard about the floods in Beruba—three hundred thousand people homeless, thousands killed.

"They'll do something. Someone will do something."

"Is there somewhere you can send a dollar?"

My friend laughed and told them there was no such country. Then the drivers laughed with him.

If Americans hear about difficulties in some other place, they feel uneasy about how well they have it and they offer help.

But, you know, you do not have it easy here. Life is not arranged for living. In Vietnam, practically every wife has other women to help her raise the children. A mother, an aunt, a servant. Almost every household has hired help. And relatives. Most of the men work close to their homes and friends. We seem to have much

69

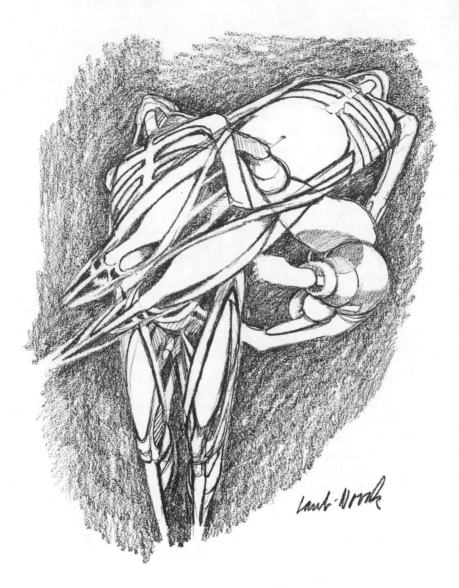

more time for ritual (ritual is very important, most of the enjoyment of life comes from ritual) and to amuse ourselves. Our lives are more quiet than yours. We are known as a happy people.

Americans are very generous. But you also have a strange isolation, separation, loneliness. One notices it immediately

In Vietnam, people are hard. I remember when the Buddhist monk burned himself, many, even Buddhists, laughed and made jokes. When I fought with the Viet Minh, it sometimes happened that we went to a village and asked the men to volunteer. The colonel asked the first man in line. He hesitated and the colonel shot him. It was a serious revolution. If you say the word "revolution," you must be ready for the logic of a certain cruelty. My people can be very hard.

In America, you are hard in a different way. In private lives, for one thing, there seems to be a great deal of cruelty. You hurt one another often. But there is a remarkable openness to strangers, a willingness to change your views. We notice it everywhere. On the other hand, the system of life is very hard—not at all on the human scale. An expressway, an airport, even the streets of Washington or New York or Chicago. It is as if Americans do not know one another, or trust one another, or cohere. There is a fatalism in the face of "progress." You allow things to be done to you. Your private ways of life are disrupted year by year and you do not complain. By automobiles and their necessities. By television. By corporations and factories and national networks of various kinds.

In Vietnam, we live on a village scale. Even in Saigon, even in Hanoi. In America, you live on an almost national scale.

The average Vietnamese, I think, is more proud of himself than the average American.

71

In America one sees so many strumming thumbs, strumming, strumming. And nervous feet—legs crossed, feet bobbing up and down. And nervous gestures of many kinds. You are not a calm people. Emotions sweep across your faces—not necessarily real emotions or deep emotions. (A foreigner learns not to trust them.)

But you do have a spontaneous generosity. I think you are the most peculiar nation in that respect. You are as a people more generous than your politicians have found a way to express.

You have easily been led into a rather missionary attitude, which is against your fundamental spirit. Once you imagine something to be evil, you are *totally* against it. That is a new, American form of totalism.

Many say now that America is corrupt, the system is evil, the government is an instrument of Death. If many of you turn upon America the same total hatred that others in America turn upon Communism, you have not made progress.

You will notice that the North Vietnamese have never insulted your traditions or your people—no, not even your government. They take the attitude that temporary arrogance, blindness, and stubbornness have perverted what your nation has been, is, will be.

No people is perfect. Vietnamese do not boast about everything that happens among us. Nor about our "system," South or North.

A people that does not love itself cannot love others.

Life is full of evils, illusions, and suffering. Why, then, are Americans surprised when it is so?

You are too surprised by evil in yourselves. Far too surprised. You give it too much importance, more than it deserves.

Twenty-Two

Fire. Emotions fire. Is love a fire? In married love, truth is fire.

To K I am grateful for insistence. She is herself. Other. She does not bend to my fantasies. About myself, she does not share illusions. Being with her is being forced to see painful truths. A white fire leaps forth, fire igniting fire. It burns away what ought to be burned.

How valuable is a marriage! In a celibate life, how atomic and enclosed I could have been. Heart in a locket, never opened. The transition from atom to molecule is a change in being. Marriage is not a legal fiction. Two become one. The fission, if genuine, is not without pain. To live one must die.

The old advice about "sacrifice"—"sacrifice yourself for the other"—is awesomely misleading. Marriage, it is true, is not aimed at "happiness." Its purpose is not escape from loneliness. Nor a solution to the dilemmas of being. Its point is a transformation.

In marriage, two people change, are transformed. From being separate, they become communal. Not merely that they share things—space, table, income, tasks, and bed. Rather, that they swiftly hold truth up to each other. Expose each other's pretensions. Jangle each other's insecurities. Unerringly discover each other's human weaknesses, even grotesqueries.

Human beings are not gods. Each is clay.

Marriage is the institution of fiery flame that clay cannot withstand. Everyone screams, and many crack.

The truth about ourselves is precious ore.

Not for "the other" do we lay "self" down in sacrifice (expecting reciprocity). For the truth about each other each sacrifices everything.

And by some unknown chemistry, humans do not easily discover truth about themselves in isolation. To become ourselves, we require such searing mutuality as neither acquaintanceship nor friendship can supply. We require a unitive force, a sexual force, a force of such vulnerability and power as only lifelong commitment to one of opposite sex supplies.

Men and women grow up in different "cultures"— masculine culture, feminine culture. And in different familial traditions. And they bring to marriage senses of reality, personal voyages, and cherished symbols that necessarily clash. For in the beginning they are not one, but two.

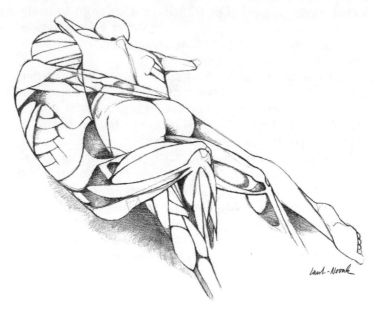

Thus marriage is a long-term affair. On the first night of marriage, the couple is not as thoroughly one as five years later they may be, or ten, or thirty.

Marriage is a commitment to grow together. It is not a commitment of me-as-I-am-now to you-as-you-are-now. But, rather, of me to you, and you to me, as we face the unknown ahead; jointly pursuing further growth in truth, that truth not revealed to one alone but only to selves-as-communal. Truth that may destroy.

For God himself, the "Really Real," the "Being Supreme," *Actus Purus* (as the classics say), has revealed himself not as single but as mutuality. God is not an atomic self. He is a Trinity.

75

Marriage is fired by God when it is participation of each in the other. *Ubi caritas et amor ibi Christus est.* In secular words: honest truth is the fire of community, the core of marital unity. Honest truth requires that each be each, separate, distinct, independent, interdependent, two yet one.

Undergoing a ceremony is not being married. Undergoing fire . . .

Twenty-Three

Freedom to write of joy has been taken from us in America. The advertisers, the promoters, the salesmen, the merchants of uplift, have devalued the language of affirmation.

How can one avoid sounding like a greeting card, or an ad for a bank?

How can one avoid sounding like a patriotic Republican in an election year?

And, therefore, my pen falls unwillingly limp against my fingers when I want it to record the surprises of marriage, the joy of children, the pleasure of coming home —the noises of our house, its silences, its terrors. (For when can I be sure it will not be taken away . . . our precarious grip unable to lock it here? . . .)

Our best writers picture marriage drab . . . I can see all the ways in which it is. As a species of political contestation . . . and it is. As a never-ending round of routine, bickering, nagging, and cruel incompatibility . . . Agreed, husband and wife put one another through the wringers of every petty emotion, named and unnamed.

But those who know that human beings are not gods, who do not seek escape from the pettiness and weariness of being who they are, who are not shocked that each is what each is, are even in knowing the worst reduced to silence . . . for the worst is but a truth within a truth.

And of the larger truth, one cannot in America truthfully speak. Like dank earth, the "boosters" rot its pillars and its posts.

Twenty-Four

Fire! In America, millions of persons have no religious experience, cherish even a tradition of hostility toward religion, believe that belief in God is puerile, hypocritical, deceptive . . .

How shall I speak, then, not of my belief in God . . . but of the burning, deep, lasting love that unaccountably I find within myself, a love for Him as deep as I may look? Joy in honesty, pleasure in a difficult but truthful words, cool refreshment in an act of courage— whenever I see anything beautiful, true, good, my heart —despite myself—leaps . . . as if then I am truly alive, and that life is God's . . . as if then we are one.

And not as if these things *are* God . . . but signs of him . . . as white heat in an ingot is a sign . . .

All nature is a Heraclitean fire . . . ingot, rather . . . God, not nature, is the fire . . .

Such silence flames induce!

Twenty-Five

Change and motion: the grey, tight branches of the maples are regaining their resilience. Hard tiny buds swell. In a few days, blossoms will break forth.

Yesterday, police cars surrounded our neighborhood. Busy Bayville Avenue was blocked off. A stranger stabbed a man on the street of our neighbors. Thick red blood. A helicopter helped find the man down along the water, on the grounds of an abandoned estate.

We saw a handsome blond dog struck by a Chevy Nova coming toward us. The Nova stopped with the dog underneath the right wheel. The dog yelped and struggled, pinned by the rubber tire. The woman tried to drive forward, dragging the dog. We waved frantically. Confused, she finally backed up. Sprung free, the dog cried out and limped speedily away, in troubled pain.

A branch that had sheltered the avenue for thirty years resignedly gave way before the eighty-mile gusts of a March storm. Twenty-seven trees in the township, that have lived here longer than almost any of the residents, were reported down, across homes and streets.

Our children grow so quickly.

Try as I might, short of a diet, I can't lose weight.

Week by week, the expressway changes. Now they are replacing the cyclone wire between the lanes with a slanting concrete wall: miles and miles.

The old estate I mentioned is being parcelled out for homes. Eighty thousand dollars for those fronting on the Sound. Quiet bridle paths, where horses once cantered, still tunnel beneath the trees that are left.

And if they put in the Oyster Bay-Connecticut bridge, right over our heads (or perhaps, as one plan shows, through our living room), what shall we do? What will our area become?

We live near farms, and luxurious estates, and squalid but friendly little towns, mixes of executives and teachers and electricians and plumbers and workmen of every sort. Almost rural towns, in which people know people.

And the Sound! Glistening water. Blue, shimmering. The cries of gulls. Sails bob and dip. The great yachts of the yachting club . . . walking on the sand, thinking of Gatsby. Yes, even of General George Washington and his wintered troops.

How like a dream it seems. The generations come and go. The newspapers overwhelm us. We had to stop them, for nausea: drowning, dizzy, buried under print. *The New York Times* and *Newsday*, both: two pounds of obligation every day.

Can all the effort of putting out all those papers, and all those radio stations, and all those television channels —can all that effort be justified?

For what do we get through the news? Information? Ah no! Stories, symbols, myths. We are fed a picture, a set of parables, morality plays. On any matter that I know at first hand, the newspaper account is rather like a tale told by Tacitus or Pliny: it would not satisfy a professional historian, its point is to interest and to instruct.

We are overburdened with storytellers, drenched in myth, and call it reality.

Why are we alive? What is the point of instruction? The point is to change one's way of life. A very hard saying. To change one's way of life. But how could I do

that? Sell everything and give it to the poor? Change my way of life?

Perhaps if I were poor—willingly poor—there would be more silence, time would pass less quickly, there would be a little less illusion.

The project of modernity, of progress, of enlightenment, of cities and commerce and technology, is illusory. Underneath it, behind it, ready to swallow it, an abyss.

I do not hate the city, or modernity, or progress. It is only that I hunger for fewer illusions: I trust living things, pain, blood, death, the tides washing a disfigured rubber doll ashore and relinquishing a thousand tiny oysters to the gulls . . .

81

Water

Limpid pool. Clear and cool to slake a desert thirst.
Honesty, humility, oceanic stirrings of festering,
primeval, multiplying Life.
Dripping from loins, blood racing through the
veins, and juices nourishing the trees.
In the heat the hart pants, the doe athirst; broken
cisterns in the sand.

Twenty-Six

Fuck, she says. *Fuck*. How I love that word. It has come to be so beautiful to me. Sometimes, making love, a sudden suction. FUCK! it says. Exactly like that. FUCK. Onomatopoeia of love.

There are times when lovemaking falls very flat, when it is a torment, when force, manipulation, anger, resentment, weariness, and a thousand emotions drain unity away. The drying up of conversation withers the act of love.

If to love were to plunge a plug into a socket, if it were mechanical, marriages would not die. Marriages die (among so many ways!) because lovemaking is symbolic. What happens in the emotions, what happens in the soul—these are indispensable. Novelty and circumstance are substitutes for soul; the excitement they bring, and the escape, make up for lack of soul.

What do I mean by "soul"? I do not mean romance merely, nor good will, nor realistic attitudes. I mean limpidity, being "present" to, being altogether with, being connected. Each person carries a world of meaning, affect, and imagined story; each is living out a story. Lovemaking is a union of touch, sensation, bodily openness and exploration and excitement: the circuit is completed if what happens to our bodies is metaphor for what happens to our worlds of meaning.

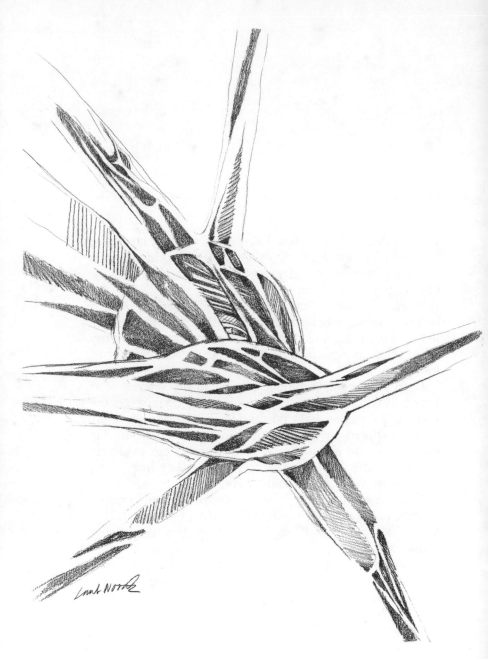

86

These are not laws I am laying down—everyone knows that a disjunction between body and world of meaning can be a pleasant, even a helpful, escape. Romantic escapades, affairs, and the more civilized forms of prostitution are institutions of great antiquity. A shipboard romance can be exciting exactly in proportion as the two worlds of meaning do not thoroughly interpenetrate.

To bring worlds of meaning together—connections of nerve ends, memories, paths of emotion, labyrinths of instinct, immensely complex chains of sensibility, tracks of imagination, circuits of expectation—is a task so fearful lifetimes are dedicated to it.

Marvelous it is to make love. (Imagine a world in which it were absent.) More marvelous still when it is love that is made.

To love, to be loved: do you know anyone who is certain that he (she) loves, is loved, truly? Anyone who loves, is loved, enough? Who has no more to explore, to learn?

It seems, rather, that many doubt that love occurs. It is the most pervasive doubt: perhaps I have never loved, cannot love, am not loved . . .

Many doubt it.

Twenty-Seven

What dehydration of soul makes organization possible? The spirit of a practical society is a bureaucratic spirit, fascinated by process, procedures, methods.

It is true, of course, that procedures affect the content of what is done. Sometimes they determine the content completely.

But it is not true that if you attend only, or even chiefly, to questions of process, procedures, and methods, you can guarantee results.

Thinking about procedures has a single goal: routine. Once we get the process down (we think), we can produce many similar contents rationally and efficiently.

At its worst, process thinking tends to imagine a world organized like a machine. It is production-line thinking.

At its best, it remains thinking from-outside-in. It views content as what is to be shaped. It concentrates on the shaping procedures. Powerful in dealing with machines, in dealing with humans it is incompetent.

For example, democracy. Many seem to imagine that democracy is a matter of machinery: who votes, when; parliamentary rules and reforms; methods for identifying interests; procedures for reconciling interests; mechanisms for handling grievances. Even radical thinkers concentrate on processes.

One can identify process thinkers early by the meta-

phors inseparable from their thinking: "Set it up," "We
need a mechanism," "Operationalize that," "Figure out
the best procedures," "Sort out the elements," "Break
it down into smaller steps," "How to structure the com
mittee," "Once we get it going it will take care of itself,"
"The problem is the procedure," "Inputs," "Outputs,"
"Crank it up with," "Safety valves . . ."

Process thinkers sound like auto mechanics on their
day off.

It seldom occurs to process thinkers—to our elites in
the intellectual and managerial classes—that democracy
requires qualities of soul, in persons and in their families,
and in their social groups.

If you reduce humans to atomic particles without social cohesion, without social trust, without joy in sacrifice, without social pride, democracy disintegrates.

If you reduce human atomic particles to inputs, outputs, and mechanisms of need and desire, democracy
becomes an illusory dream machine and its springs snap,
bolts fall off, panels rot away, organisms rust and decay
. . . the machine ceases to function.

Democracy is not a matter of reasonable discussion
merely, of intelligent consensus, of the decorum of a
New England town meeting *circa* 1663. It includes pressure groups, interest groups, conflicts, the use of force,
threats, bitter dissent.

But where persons are not proud of their own lives,
independent and sturdy in their views, committed to
mutual trust in their morals, larger police forces are
needed. Suburban communities become, like medieval
towns, walled cities. People go out seldom. No one
evinces pride in work or workmanship. Each person
takes what he can get, and gives a minimum. Transactions between salesgirls and customers, between agents
and clients, are reduced to the most minimal mechanical
forms: a grunt, a reluctant gesture of direction. Cold

hostility intensifies between busdrivers and passengers, servicemen and homeowners, mechanics and auto owners. Surliness and contempt multiply. Citizens trust no government official. Officials are cynical about the people.

Where private and familial and occupational habits turn from cooperative to mistrustful, democracy dies. Not all the processes or procedures or methods in the world, even if enforced by penalties and arms, can hold a society together.

The radical disease of American life lies in a quarter no one wishes to face. Everyone wants to tinker with the system. More profound is the collapse of personal and social virtue. Humility, graciousness, warmth, trust, spontaneity, and generosity of soul are disappearing slowly but steadily from our lives. We are not humane in the small transactions of daily life. We do not, in fact, love, sympathize with, or trust most of the human beings we meet each day. We are on our guard. They, too, are on their guard.

If we become a garrison state, the sole cause will not be an industrial-military complex. Truly, if our major corporations mass-produced marshmallows instead of sophisticated weaponry, the impact of mass-production and bureaucracy would be the same: the disease of thinking from-outside-in.

A society is humane if and only if the dominant note of its private, familial, and societal transactions is reverence for what other persons are suffering: respect for thinking from-inside-out.

Each human is already lonely, trapped in the coils of his (her) own ego, unhappy, silently in pain. If you assume that this is true of each person you meet, seldom will events prove you mistaken. Why, then, would you add to the enormous weight of pain which grinds into their shoulders?

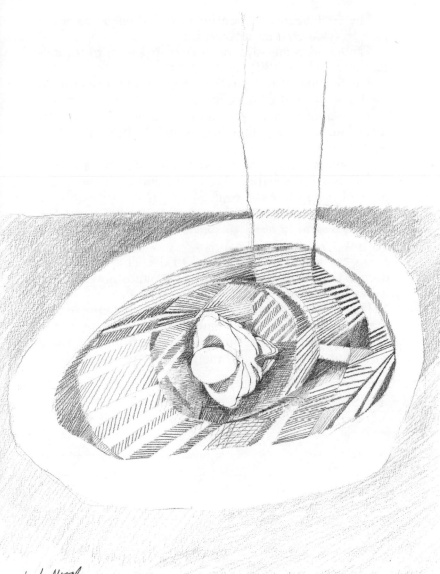

The dry bureaucratic sentiment is: Design a procedure that every one has an interest in.

The liquid democratic sentiment is: Listen to the suffering of each, and lift the burdens.

The bureaucrat trusts administration. His way of making law is to fund an agency.

The democrat relies on himself and mutual trust. His way of making law is to articulate an ideal that men will agree to live under, cooperatively.

The bureaucrat worries about sanctions and administrators and investigators. He is not entirely wrong. But he tends to neglect the soul.

Dissent in order to begin a new way of life is not the same as dissent in order to spread contempt, hatred, and distrust.

Dissent which does not lead to deeper sympathy, to deeper sinking down of roots, is a sandstorm beating leaves from living trees.

The contrast, William James wrote, is between the "soft" thinkers and the "hard." More accurate is the contrast between those in whom juices run, and those who think only where arid methodology permits.

Twenty-Eight

Cong Hoa Speaks:
You cannot hang leaders of Germany and leaders of Japan, and then according to identical principles ignore the leaders of your own nation.

Men in command do not know every incident that takes place in the field. But, in difficult circumstances, what precautions did they take? War encourages terrorism and brutality. What have they done to mitigate them? Too little? Did all their encouragement run in a dangerous direction?

We are sensitive to such questions, we Vietnamese. We are not tall and white. We are not a people oriented to machines and technology. We are not skilled at administration. We do not speak English. For all these reasons, and many more, we are accustomed to the exasperation and the contempt in which our American friends hold us. Do not think we do not feel, with our stomachs, what Americans feel as they talk to us and talk about us.

Your deeds exemplify your feeling.

We are but a people of sixteen millions. We do not fight wars as you fight them. Will you forgive me if, from time to time, I cannot wholly master the tears that burn my eyes?

Boys from Kansas were not trained to defoliate the

93

fields of farmers, or to throw dead animals into village wells, or to herd women and children into trucks . . . Perhaps a generation hence, Americans will begin to learn what young men did in Vietnam.

It is known already in their uneasy consciences, in their silent memories.

The emotions of destruction will come out in ten million midnight screams, a thousand million evil dreams.

You will one day want to purge your soul.

At that time, it will be easy to become vindictive. Those who opposed the war will try to maintain the proud eyes of the pure. Did many in the anti-war movement think less of the Vietnamese dying day by day

than of their own hatred for "middle America"? The anti-war movement became a discharge of bitter domestic emotion.

To Americans, perhaps, "moral" means that the moral man is superior to the immoral one. To us, in our underdeveloped way, that is moral which, in harmony with the universe, knits together the souls of all people. "Moral" means "unitive."

War crime trials in America, therefore, may be the opposite of moral. They may be divisive. They may be a means by which one part of the population tries to prove its superiority over another.

North and South Vietnam, Catholics and Buddhists, A.R.V.N. and N.L.F. We have much to forgive one another.

Perhaps reconciliation is not possible, in one land, or among all lands.

Why, then, do the stars decree it? The same stars that shine on all of us, all of us underneath the stars . . .

Twenty-Nine

There are many reasons why a tragic sense of life does not come easily to Americans, and why a tragic sense of life is required if we are not to destroy ourselves. Until recently it was so easy not to believe evil of ourselves. Even when we saw the photographs used as evidence in the Calley trial, it was easy to be detached from them. They could not have connection to us.

To begin with, we were a new nation, born on a new continent, a people eager to forget past human history.

For three and a half centuries we have had to believe that Americans are "a good people." That belief has been a necessary pillar of our sense of worth and meaning.

We had to believe that America would be hope. America would be beautiful. America would be "new."

What would be newest about it would be the absence of tragedy. Optimism became the one necessary foundation of the republic. Things must always be looking up.

Even when our children despair of us, it is not from despair. It is from too much hope. So powerful is the American illusion that our children are absorbed by it, and are full of rage not because their parents preached illusion, but because their parents failed to live up to it.

We see now, after three hundred and fifty years, that such ideological blinders prevented our ancestors—and ourselves—from recognizing the true history of our nation and its true relation to the rest of the world.

The new world became hopelessly enmeshed in slavery and its deep psychic corruptions, which would entangle human relations as tragically as ever they had been in "the old world." In aggrandizement, greed, chicanery, and exploitation, the men of the new world showed daily that the new history was all too like the old. Enormous advantages of a fresh beginning in a wealthy and beautiful land were all too quickly squandered.

The atom bomb was dropped on cities crowded with men of the yellow race. Torture, assassination, murder, and an unparalleled scorching of the land came to characterize, to an extent not yet explored, American tactics in a war full of dilemmas in Vietnam.

The artificiality of an economy based on advertising causes many men and women of sensitivity muted anguish in their daily work—was it this that in their youth they had in mind as "fulfillment"? Public duty and private escape divide the lives of many.

Had Americans a tragic sense, none of this would be surprising. What is more typical of the human story than such a denouement? Had we a tragic sense, we could perhaps admit military and political defeats, admit that "the heart of America" is not particularly good but ambivalent, admit that our public and private lives are shot through with falsehood and betrayal.

Nothing more common and ordinary than that. It is, rather, the pretense of innate goodness that so bitterly divides Americans. Since each must think of himself or herself as good, it becomes necessary to project evil on the others.

Thus middle Americans blame "agitators" and "Communists," radicals blame "pigs" and "fascists," black militants blame "honkies" and "imperialists," women's lib blames "men," liberals blame "ideologues."

97

The tragic sense of life suggests that the plague is not in others but in ourselves. It suggests that all things human, given enough time, go badly. And it does not find in such suggestions reason for shock, or crippling feelings of guilt, or dismay, or escape from action. On the contrary, the tragic sense of life differs from pathos precisely because it views humans as agents and actors, not as victims.

The tragic sense of life is a calm acceptance of despair, a firm determination to act well and unflinchingly, and forgiveness in advance for others and for oneself. No one escapes the burden of being fully human—even when each well knows himself to be incompletely human.

Tragedy arises precisely because we are called upon to act today with a wisdom, courage, honesty, and compassion we do not as yet possess. Had our people and our leaders a tragic sense of life, America would be less self-flagellant, more at peace with herself, and far less pretentious among others. Expecting less, we might quietly do more. Less righteous, we might be more honest with ourselves and with each other.

Thirty

Tears, conflict, and anguish: Problems of authority in dealing with our children. Most of my life, I stood *under* authority. It is different now. *I* must decide. I must also choose the tone and manner of my decision. Is it "No" or "NO!"?

How much children understand emotionally. Their range isn't vast, but otherwise their emotions are equal to those of an adult. When we are at peace in the home, they tend to be. If we are troubled, they become cranky. Their emotions are good barometers. When they cry, are fussy, quarrel, whine, we examine our own conduct— and also their situation. A bad morning at nursery school leads at home to many crises.

Our children love to talk about emotions. Anger, especially, fascinates them. Books and stories that dramatize anger, loneliness, fear of loss, farewells, they greet with pleasure and glowing eyes. Also jealousy, rivalries, selfishness, failure, competitiveness, impoliteness—articulations of their experiences. They mimic these emotions. Sometimes they read a feeling or a glance and ask: "Are you lonely, Daddy?" Or, "Are you happy now?"

It has been astonishing to trace the contours of emotions they experience. Perhaps in highly cultivated families, where for three generations parents have college courses in child psychology, such things are well known,

A Lonely, Happy, Angry Kitten   BY RICHARD NOVAK   (age 5)

I have had to learn the hard way—and the delightful way.

To work at explaining how the three-year-old boy isn't obliged to *love* his baby sister, he can hate her if he wants to; but please don't hit her, because she's too little. Hit Tuffy (the inflated clown) if he needs to hit.

Someone told me something very simple. Bringing a new baby home is for the older child like bringing a new mistress home to meet your wife. "Alice, this is Helen. She'll be living with us now. Don't worry, though. I still love you, we *both* love you, I love you both equally."

It's too much, asking children to love one another. They have plenty of reason to resent one another.

They seem to enjoy "sharing" things. If one has a toy, find one for the other. And "trading."

Children are totally egocentric. Selfish, quickly hostile, violent. They seem willing to enjoy bringing others into their ego's center, however.

Assume that children are totally oriented toward their own needs for food, warmth, emotional comfort. Granting that, one can see how legitimate are many of the things they do. Still, it would be betrayal to allow them to continue manipulating people and events to their needs. The task—how arduous!—is to find ways for them to enjoy "sharing," "cooperating," "being gentle," "not quitting," "trying again," and so on.

Fear is easily misused; and delight is a better teacher anyway.

How capable a bright child is of diagnosing my own weaknesses, better than I can, pushing me with absolute finesse into every corner of my character. Testing, probing, pushing . . . it is a constant battle. Often with my own exasperation.

At a very early age, not too many negatives in their path. Move out of the room anything they shouldn't get into. And then just a few clear and solid "no's": electrical cords, the street.

But as they pass two and move toward three, it becomes more important to learn how to say "No" in ways quick, firm, and non-negotiable. As often as possible with reasons given. (Our children seem to love hearing reasons for things; their eyes are attentive; they retain reasons long afterwards.) Sometimes, with no reason except that Daddy or Mommy say so. Authority, for authority's sake, is, first of all, a good thing for children to learn—but not to overlearn.

I do not believe that life is, or should be, wholly reasonable; it is well to learn early how to make do within limits. On the other hand, the appeal to "Daddy said so" is a sign of weakness, at least if used too frequently. Children do not give reasons for all their wants, claims, and demands; some irrationality on Daddy's part is fair play. The task of giving reasons is often more fatiguing than it's worth.

The point is—perhaps everyone in the world knew it but me—there is relaxation and relief in children when parents stand firm. Our children, at least, seem to thrive once they have discovered the limits. They seem happier when I do not give in, than when I do. (I like to try both ways. Sometimes, of course, the kids are right and I was wrong in my first decision. In decisions that could go either way, I've learned it's better for them if I am firm.) They understand quite well the realities of the situation: I am bigger and stronger, they are extraordinarily vulnerable. So plain is this fact that it does not need proof. All it needs is fidelity. Willy-nilly, authority is mine, no escaping it.

My children and I are not, cannot be, "friends"—that is to say, equals. Our relationship is, must always be, one of inequality. Emotionally, my power to hurt them, or to make them proud of themselves, is beyond my control or my will; the only choice I have is how to exercise such power. The power is there.

Profound wavering on the question of power. I seem to have been taught to fear it, to deny that I have it, to allow its exercise to be as unconscious as possible, to strive to replace relations of power by relations of equality, community, fraternity. Fraternalism is a good word; paternalism is a vice.

Finding myself a father, I face paternalism as a fact. And it turns out not to be such an evil fact. Learning how to be a good father is one of those things one must, it seems, learn by instinct and experiment; few are the gestures of social assistance, in school or elsewhere.

Every fault of mine I begin to see affecting my children. If I grow angry (and I do, suddenly, furiously, in the stormy European way), I worry that the irrationality of it will encourage irrationalities of their own. It does.

On the other hand, if I am preternaturally calm, they see through the disguise—they read the unspoken emotion under the reasonableness. I am fairly certain that they do.

It is surely true that they enjoy laughing when I explain my dilemma and switch from anger to amusement by way of despair.

No one prepared me for how much fun my children would be. Nor for how much I would learn about my own emotions and ambivalences. Ambivalences running back to experiences with my own parents, and even to their experiences with their parents; ambivalences in myself, because of the different cultural streams making up my own emotional life.

I am, after all, of peasant and petit-bourgeois origin, of conservative European stock; I am a Catholic, with a profound love of the ancient past; and most of the cherished values in my educational liberation derived from the Enlightenment and from contemporary humanistic sources. Many ambivalences here. Not all the merit on one side.

A Book of Elements

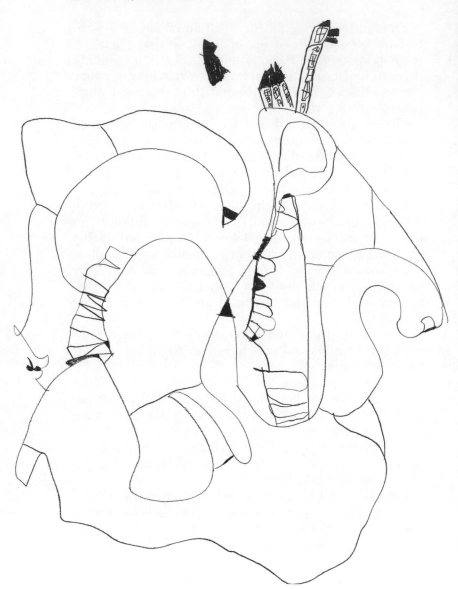

The Road to Our House BY TANYA NOVAK (age 4)

No wonder it is difficult for me to speak with one clear mind to my children. I am, at the very least, one man in three distinct persons, trinity of disharmony and complication.

How will they judge me thirty years from now?

Thirty-One

Is it wrong to love to work in the garden? Dreadfully suburban. Intellectual friends visit and notice that we have a stationwagon, bushes from the nursery poking out the windows, a red wheelbarrow in the yard. How can I explain?

Or a large color TV in the livingroom, for pro football games—and the morning re-broadcast of (hold your breath) Notre Dame games.

Shamelessly suburban.

The pleasures I derive from digging up the lawn and gathering thick dirt underneath my fingernails are worth the shame of it. The cool earth clings to my clothes, and you could probably plant a row of ferns in the dirt I annually carry to my room in pants cuffs and on shoes. . . . Paint brush in hand . . . bending nails . . . raising blisters on my hands . . . The air, the sky, branches sweeping against the silver hot sun, sweat running down my back . . . burning in the corners of my eyes . . . Tying a birdhouse to a branch twice my height above the ground . . . digging deep holes for fence posts . . . On such a tiny lot that all this must sound extravagant, and yet the house is old and things are always going wrong; the lawn is (was) virtually non-existent; the old trees required pruning, and new bushes were needed for price-less privacy . . .

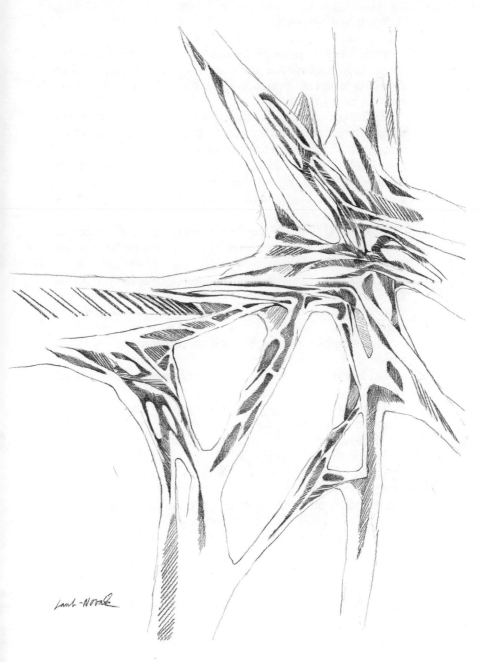

Laul-Novak

Such work is perhaps as near to prayer as I can get these days. Compared to hours in the office, it is like drinking long cool draughts of water . . . or cold sweating cans of beer in August . . .

And playing squash, the thick odors of the men's locker room . . . Socks so sweaty they are ready to get up and walk . . . water running and everlastingly dripping . . . And the good clean sweat breaking out upon my back as we hurry around the white gleaming court, dizzy, as in a dream, *slam, slam, slam,* run and swing, retreat to cover, over, up, back . . .

Humble things, in my experience, are the center of life. To know when we have them, and not to run too hard . . .

It is, I know, shameless to have a home, television, time for lawns and sports, and beer . . . shameless in a world of poverty and misery . . . or else . . . or else perhaps not so.

More crucial by far to find contentment, to be at peace. It is not inner peace that breeds the evils of the world but restlessness . . . I wish I could convince myself of that.

There is a nagging guilt. I have seen such streets as must be terrors to be confined upon . . . smelled the piss on the stairwells of tenements . . . watched the faces in the open windows in the steaming heat of July . . . seen, too, the scabs of dirt on children's heads in jungle villages . . .

How does one put together a private and a public life? Restore the spirit, and also assume responsibility for the reconstruction of a world in which all human beings share such goods?

Guilt is not an emotion I like to encourage in myself. Suburban life, however, has a contradiction established at its heart. There is in it such prospect for peace, such resources for deepening the spirit—not in gregariousness, not in friendly neighbors and ice cubes clinking in glasses of scotch, not in the country club (those rituals of community, celebrating no Mystical Body but an afternoon's camaraderie), not in the Kaffee Klatches . . . no, but in a bit of soil, a touch of privacy, a surcease from busyness, a place into which to withdraw . . .

In such a way, the suburb becomes an image refracted around this planet in countless ways: an approach to a simpler life, a touch of village life, a retreat to primitive times . . . Its point is not its gimmicks (outdoor lighting, a pool, a patio) but its inner strengthening . . .

Nearly all "radicals"—the readers, indeed the editors and reviewers of this book—are middle class. It is the one title, however, no one wishes to be called.

Every writer I know is middle class: loves cocktails, cheeses, wines, a summer place, travel, "bread" for books. The style is Continental. The money that it takes is American.

One of my favorite revolutionaries is even now on a grant in Majorca, writing a book on revolution. How many kidnapings and draft-card raids are discussed at summer homes . . . how much money is required for a good education, for time to think—and to politick . . .

Suburban life can be the death of spirit. Or rebirth. The hope of the world is the middle class.

For a whole week to do nothing but sit in a rocking chair, ruminating. Then, in the second week, slowly to begin rocking . . .

"Don't just do something. Stand there."

(To cite Daniel Berrigan, who walks within the walls of a prison as I write.)

Thirty-Two

Modern man, some people say, can no longer believe in God. So many things modern man can no longer do.

Ditto for post-modern man.

There are not, however, very many modern or post-modern humans. And, in any case, dissent is still an honorable profession. No one needs to be intimidated by the spirit of his age. No one lives less because he is not in step with the common wisdom of his time and place.

It is astonishing how many layers of civilization live among us and in each of us . . . in how many cultures we each partake.

One of the privileges of life today is to be many men at once, planetary men almost, deriving nourishment from here and there, then and now, afterwards and before, tomorrow and yesterday . . .

One God, one light, one spirit, one belt of inspiration uniting all men who are, were, will be, one seamless net of (Dostoevsky's word) humble charity . . .

Humble: truthful, without pretense, in touch with earth (*humus*); without ornament or wax or defensiveness; limpid, clear: oneself.

Charity: realistic love of others, one's center not in oneself but encompassing all humans in one single blazing center, as they are and not as we might wish them to be, in themselves and not because of what they might be useful for . . .

If a person lives in truth, such humbleness, such charity, characterize his actions. One finds such persons everywhere. And there are, in truth, no persons who do not implicitly testify to the power of humble charity. For all despise hypocrisy (in others) and have contempt for egocentrism . . . All? Perhaps Ayn Rand will argue that it is more *true* to announce one's egotism and have the courage to live accordingly . . . Sadly, there are many who do not "testify," either in word or in deed, to humble charity. They are not, for all that, less in need of our respect for who they are and what they are . . .

Humans are not to be trusted. (One does not even trust oneself.) "No one is a judge in his own case." "Self-love dies fifteen minutes after death." A person who at all times and in all places voices nothing but the truth (there is no such person) would be put to death or treated as an idiot. Human affairs are not so constituted as to withstand the withering truth: only a little truth.

One must not assume, then, that humans are fundamentally good, that everyone has good will, that there are no such phenomena as deliberate lying and malice and corruption. One must know very little of one's own complexities of heart to believe that humans are inherently honest, brave, and true. An honest man, surely, knows that he lies seven times a day. Among university professors, among psychiatrists, flattery is more easily believed, less critically assessed, than optimism would suggest.

Let us assume that humans seldom live up to their capacities, even under the most favorable conditions. An assumption that observation of human life has in all places and in all times taught those who are least surprised by events.

To be sure, if one expects a great deal from people, many are more likely to live up to expectations. Thus the truth comes out: For good human performance, many supports are needed. And in most places, at most times, over the long run, these are not provided. Humans are left naked in their freedom. And they betray themselves.

Think for a moment of all the persons nearest you. How far below their potential they still live. How hard they struggle this year to develop some little further beyond where they were last. How many faults, deficiencies, inhibitions, tendencies, habits they will never overcome.

Those who begin by trusting the good will and the future development of men are most likely to despair: of their own petty progress, of those most entangled in their lives, of their nation, and the race. Unless they learn to think ideologically. And imagine some other world, under some other social system, in some other time.

Beware of those who love men because men are good. If on so fundamental a point they see so foggily, the future toward which they speed us bears promise not of compassion but of elimination. When they have cut out all that is wrong with the human race, in accordance with the pattern laid up in their heads, only the mutilated will survive.

It is no sign of compassion to trust in human goodness. Self-betrayal and betrayal of those one loves are ever-present possibilities. It is not charity to believe that men are good. It is a form of blindness.

Charity is compassionate. It suffers-with. It loves men as they are: of ambivalent heart and free.

Thirty-Three

In medieval paintings, children are small adults. There is no time of life special to childhood.

The Enlightenment invented childhood. Industrial society invented adolescence. Today we are inventing twentyhood: ten extra years during which one can, with a little help from adult society, evade marital and economic responsibility until thirty or so. The energy and attention of society tend to be transfixed upon its own favorite age.

What has happened, meanwhile, to children in America? Many are, of course, treated with more respect for their individuality and more sense of their personal dignity than at any time in history. Many others seem to be emotionally more neglected than at any time in history.

Mothers so often seem to resent their children; fathers seem to be busy and baffled. Casually let a mother remark to other mothers how much she enjoys her children: freeze. A father tells acquaintances he never imagined children would be such fun: silence.

The children are finally away at school: "How marvelous."

Neighborhood doors slam, children on the outside, mothers inside. If one mother likes to be with her children, she will be obliged to be babysitter for the neighborhood.

It is not as if all mothers had other things to do. It is often the very mothers who live for nothing else but children, have no other life, who are the most resentful. Such mothers are not cruel. Victims, perhaps—feeling that they must be mothers, finding their identity in that, and feeling the years slip away from them. A round of household duties, television, a magazine or two, the pets. And painful, burning, hidden inner rage.

Is there no way of reaching all the mothers of the land? Inviting them to grow, learn skills, take risks, feel pride in their development? When mothers give two hours to the children, let those hours be the good ones —teaching their children skills, helping them to grow. There is far more pleasure in stimulating children than in "minding" them. Children thirst for knowledge, are immensely capable of understanding, grasping, and learning more today than they knew yesterday.

As it is, adult lives are not organized around the children, nor should they be. Little children may, of course, keep their mother "prisoner." The work, too, is exhausting. But, emotionally, adult lives are not, and cannot be, centered in the children's lives. Warmth, affection, stimulation, genuine attention, serious talk—children require these. They are not God, not the center of the universe, not enough to live for. (After all, they leave.)

When adult lives are centered elsewhere, children have room to breathe. But everything depends on whether the children are taken seriously in the hours during which they share their parents' attention. Children are not, need not be, leeches or parasites. They do not suck our blood. They need emotional support; they thirst to learn and to be taught.

As the years go on, the number of children abandoned through divorce by one parent or the other never fails to grow. A ten-year-old girl cannot sleep at night because she is afraid she will lose her last remaining parent, too.

Children as burden; children as a price to pay; children as a draining responsibility; children as a drag: there is a generation gap in America, a gap in welcome and affection and reinforcement.

Parents are troubled about what to teach their children, how to bring them up. Should they teach them about God, and take them to church? Many are not certain. Should they be firm disciplinarians, or allow the children liberty? Should they entrust their children to the values of the peer group? Should they be more concerned than other parents seem to be, or let the children run with the crowd? From the tyranny of parents, children fall into the tyranny of peers.

To train children to be fiercely independent, committed to an art or craft, enamored of highest standards of taste and discrimination, is to isolate the children from the power and the slack relaxation of America— that nation, as Mencken put it, of "third-rate men," proud that they are third-rate.

The girl your high school senior class thought had "most personality"—do you remember her? Precisely the girl of no personality, oil on wheels, she *smiled* at everyone. Miss America, the sweet young thing with nothing of her own, no angularity, to jar two hundred million fantasies. Nothing as ideal: empty cheerfulness.

Thirty-Four

What is the root of our common emptiness?

The ideal is so powerful among us that life is a matter of pleasing the ego, through excitement and escape. "Get away from it all." Our enemy: routine. Uneventfulness is shameful. Made to feel guilty if our lives lack ecstasy, we are encouraged to treat every social bond as a restriction upon the questing ego.

We come to imagine that we make a great contribution to human happiness if we are not dependent upon others, nor they upon us . . . live and let live, give our children plenty of freedom, let them go. Owe no one anything. The pursuit of happiness turns out to be pursuit of loneliness.

The lack of social ties, the chill, neglect—children feel it. What we call freedom is for them restlessness, despair, resentfulness.

Every day the voices of parents humiliating children pound in upon our ears. We want to scream in pain. Yet the children know no other way of life; what is, is to them all that is possible. And yet they hunger, so many children of middle-class America, they hunger for human warmth and nourishment. They've lived alone so many years.

In place of kisses, hugs, embraces, conversations, shared silences, they are given things: flooded, drowned, with

117

clothes, money, records, toys—things. Mounds and mounds of things. Suffocation under things.

It is as if a large proportion of parents in America had lost their tongues, no longer had hearts adaptable to children, had no time or complicated counselling to share. Connections between heart and words have been torn like phone lines from a wall: sentimental stirrings cannot issue forth in speech. All one knows is how to offer money. What cannot be shown, or said, or shared, is bought.

"Here, kids, take a quarter." It used to work, when Uncle George used to do it—gruff, rough, steelworker, inarticulate, direct. Today the effect is disastrous. The aura of extended family is gone; money flows like water (hard to retain, but ever moving); and what so many of the young desire has no price: adult companionship.

The greatest human good of all is connectedness; shared emotions; shared risks; shared activities.

Middle-class Americans are culturally deprived. Things they have. Mobility they have. The price they pay is self-sufficiency, autonomy, dependence on no others. No one is needed by anyone else. The price they pay is a pervasive uselessness. No one "belongs."

The average friendship lasts two and one-half years. The average time for conversation between husband and wife: seventeen minutes a day.

Absent for three years, a friend of mine visited his father. Appropriate clichés, until the father offers: "Turn on the television?" The young man has become president of his firm, a whole world of new experience welling up inside . . . Impossible to pick up, to locate, the broken tendrils . . .

Two silent hours later: "Dad, I think I'll go to bed."
"Good to have you home, son."

Air

Elemental air: the lungs lashed. Run and run and run until the chest bursts. Heave, and collapse: a runner dies. Deep into the water dive until the ears split. Cirrus miles above the earth. Scent of pines beneath the heavy sun. Purse your lips, push outwards: Spirit, breath, creation, light, desire, aspiration, hope . . . One Earth, one air.

Thirty-Five

The American way of life disappoints. It is so shallow. What is "deep"?

Three elements of life: birth, suffering, and death. All three elements, in America, shoved aside, disguised, pushed to the edges of consciousness.

Birth: chloroform or ether or other sedatives rip birth from the consciousness of women. Hospitals have taken birth from home and family, entrusting it to white, sterile factories. Birth lives no more.

Who is alert, at birth? During pregnancy, women are ashamed. What honor is paid them? They drag through the months, worry about incipient pangs, await the sedative.

The child, too, squeezes through his mother's deadened door and into life drugged. At birth, he experiences not joy and liberation but defeat. The world that welcomes him: impersonality; chrome, metal, institutional linen; routine; internal sluggishness from drugs.

No brave, bold mother; no triumph over risk; no athletic contest fought to victory; no exhilaration or exultant jubilee: passivity, unconsciousness; swept here and there by busy strangers, amid machines.

The emotions of father and mother are in every conceivable social and institutional way diminished. Many good dollars pay for a humiliating, crowded, assembly line of bored and condescending workers.

The miracle of birth triumphs over hospitals. But such contrivances to suffocate it! What should be the center of consciousness—vivid metaphor for creativity, of triumph over time, of hope, rejuvenation, a new beginning, a fresh untrammelled slate—is dimmed.

No ritual intensifies it and recreates it. No months and years are spent in preparation for it. It is an ugly necessity, a disease, a price one has to pay . . . unless, of course, by natural childbirth and family participation one knows how to wrest pure joy from it.

* * *

Suffering? Life is not for happiness. All its beauties and its glories spring from conflict, pain, agony, and failure.

So simple a matter as a trip abroad: if smooth and well-planned what a bore. The worse things go, the more one's memory is fired. Disaster is the fuel of human growth, and growth the measure of excitement. Americans who so arrange their voyages abroad that they see nothing except America are minute-by-minute fed excitement, never a moment "dull" . . . and yet when they return have grown in moral stature not at all.

Between "killing time" and experiencing new worlds of consciousness, a poignant chasm. That difference is precisely marked: in proportion as you suffer, so you grow. If suffering breaks your shell.

The reason, too, is plain. We suffer because our world of meaning is too small. Life demands more than we expected, is absurd and dense and angular, does not fit our forms. It uproots, breaks, and smashes us. Dying, we are forced to grow.

Listen well to older persons. The more adversities they faced, the greater wisdom, joy, and delight in having lived.

The bitter, the resentful, and the bored refused to let

themselves be broken. Hardened shells, they did not grow. Therefore, they hate themselves. They wanted life to come to them and did not recognize it was their pettiness kept life out.

As the years go on, the cumulative weight of ten hundred thousand gestures, intonations, intentions, attitudes inclines the tree of character as surely as prevailing winds. The old tip in pronounced direction: there are the happy and the bitter ones. How they accepted suffering decides.

* * *

And death. How hard it is, in America, to speak of death. Not even the dying may. The doctors won't. The families can't.

Death! So clear, simple, inevitable, natural, so beautiful, so full. Ripeness ready to rush forth. For what has one lived but death? Preparing for it every day, each of which may be the last.

"Every day," said Pope John, "is a good day to die."

Whether one believes in God, or not, or doesn't care. Death is to life what sugaring is to fruit: the quintessential self, everything subsumed and gathered up, in last, climactic taste.

Eat! Drink! Dance the dance! Let the music play. Hear, the steps do come, begun at birth and nearer now: bridegroom, bride, sister-brother of my soul.

As if for every infant beginning the hourglass journey, another child begins an opposite trek: child of life, meet child of death. When one has finished, the other has arrived. They kiss.

* * *

Birth, suffering, and death. For these, humans live. All else is dissipation. Everything else diffuses energy, will never satisfy, misconstrues the elements of life.

Birth, suffering, and death are true. Whatever else may come is compounded of illusion.

124

To be "shallow" is to hold birth, suffering, and death away from consciousness.

To be "deep" is to hold them in the center of attention: one's consciousness in tune with one's reality.

To be "deep" is not to be abstruse. It is to be, on the contrary, simple, direct, and accurate.

Thirty-Six

When did character begin to disappear? Remember how stubborn, angry, ornery, crotchety, and difficult our grandparents were? The generation of complicated maiden aunts, slightly crazy uncles, and deliciously eccentric cousins has perished from the earth.

How similar we all become. How smooth, like pebbles. Organized, with watches on our wrists, studied, supervised, taught how to file the proper forms and wait in the appropriate offices, convey the proper graces, and smile pleasantly. The closer our family was to Europe, the more interesting and mad it was. The more it becomes American, the more it assumes the consistency of Pennzoil, the reliability of a light switch on the wall.

Dominant America is engaged in a vast enterprise to banish madness, neurosis, unpredictability, anxiety, and outbursts from the earth. Our air is stale. Ineluctably, systematically, relentlessly, we insist upon the normal. When at last all our people will be compatible with machines, we shall relax: all will be well.

The sacrifice is for the sake of order and prosperity. The machines will mass-produce, efficiently and cheaply, if we all behave. Would you trade a wild desire for a toaster, an idiosyncrasy for a washer and a dryer, a life of doing what you will when you will for a Buick 8? For a swimming pool? Every good citizen has his (her) price.

The meshes are working overtime. Rejecting the lumpy gravel, sending onward only those who make it through the screen. To the next bouncing, shifting mesh, along an endless conveyor belt. From nursery school to college to suburb to expense account to country club and trips to Acapulco. Yes, even the quality of one's coffin depends upon the screens one passes through.

So much the same! So similar!

One can move from coast to coast, city to city, suburb to suburb, and ever the neighbors are the same. Opinions, values, dreams, practices, foods, decors, occupations, habits—unbelievably the same.

It is not that they are stupid or even trivial. Most American neighbors are pleasant, exemplify good will, and mean well. One can be endlessly astonished at their decency.

They punish themselves too much, refusing to admire what is irrational in themselves, forcing themselves to be what they are not. They exclude the odd, the terrifying, the tragic, the incomprehensible. Has ever an entire people pretended so hard that life is reasonable, everything under control, we're happy here?

One does not need x-ray eyes to see how close to suicide some persons are. To sense the desperation behind puffs on a cigarette. To catch signals from steady drinking, sullenness, and sudden rage.

Many have been helped by the League for Irrational Behavior (LIB). LIB encourages its members to cultivate and to develop their neuroses. Evidence of difficulties they have thrown in the way of smooth adjustment is rewarded. Each year, the person who showed most signs of madness and instability, while managing to bring no physical harm on others, is elected "Irrational Man (or Woman) of the Year." [The word "irrational" defined by contrast to technological and bureaucratic Reason.]

Neurosis is a fertile field for creativity. Artists, writers, dancers, singers—perhaps even mad scientists. Why should all our nuts become generals in the Air Force?

There must be better ways of planning suburbs, mass-producing television, and distributing clothing, than by excluding craziness.

LIB gives prizes too: For the Ten Most Useless Inventions of the Year.

For the Ten Best Ways to make Mass Production unpredictable.

For the Ten Most Neurotic Couples of the Year.

For the most Volatile and Violent Shrew of the Year —and Most Feminine Man.

Every breath of air, to nourish, must be fresh.

The trick in nourishing neurosis, or insanity, or wildness, or difference does not lie in keeping it in its place, but in enlarging that place and its varieties.

Persons uncertain whether they have quirks, fears, a hidden rage, or suicidal impulses which might be turned to creative fruit should consult their wives or husbands.

* * *

A rival society to LIB is the Society for the Prevention of Normality. Each day members smash a jar of catsup, peanut butter, or anything homogenized.

One of their main aims is to make happy marriages illegal.

Argument and agony, the association contends, are indispensable to emotional adventure and moral growth.

Incompatibility is, according to the association, a precondition of mature marriages.

The irrational in each of us needs cultivation.

For what our society means by "Reason" is not what the ancients meant. Machines govern reason now. In those days, they were free—in *that* respect, at least. (Air upon this planet has never yet been free.)

Thirty-Seven

Once, coming through the medieval streets between the Tiber and St. Peter's, an American turning a corner gained suddenly his first glimpse of Michelangelo's dome. He was overpowered. Just then, a businessman from Michigan and his wife arrived. No words broke the silence until the businessman inquired: "How much does it cost to keep it lit at night?"

Artists depend on a perceptive audience as fish depend on water. Unless their audience delights in discrimination, care, and a love for craftsmanship, artists won't survive. A people conditioned to buy in supermarkets, department stores, and discount houses is not a people with a love for art.

Art is joy in the idiosyncratic, the unique, the personal, the irreplaceable.

Art is love for what cannot be mass-produced, perhaps not even translated, or transported: a statue made for a castle in Alsace may be out of place, vulgar, improper in a Texas garden.

Art depends on contingency: this vision of this artist at this time in this place.

Science is concerned with the repeatable; art with the unique.

A culture whose basic metaphor is the marketplace has a bias which blinds it to the bias of art.

To acquire an art requires a long, relentless apprenticeship. To say what she wishes to say, an artist requires a wide range of skills. During the many years required to learn her craft, the artist has nothing to sell. Meanwhile, the bills come in. A society with a high standard of living places insupportable financial pressures upon her. Art as a way of life is easier in cultures of simplicity.

In simpler cultures pleasure is taken in earthy things: biting a pear fresh from a tree, homemade cheese, the texture of the earth in fields, the sounds of one's neighborhood. Artists require a world of their own, here and now, concrete and real, in which to immerse themselves and sink their roots. A little travel, perhaps, to learn new skills and to stimulate the instincts. Imagination, and sensibility: a sharp eye for differences.

Among a people drowning in the similar, the artist feels alone. If people are happy with imitations and artificial sweeteners and truckloads of cardboard cartons bearing identical merchandise, their native discrimination bleeds away. "Seen one slum, you've seen them all." They do not understand the artist or her agony.

Their eye becomes accustomed to seeing, but never sees. Their eye detects what is practical, useful, cheap, passable. It does not notice age, uniqueness, character, signature. It seeks the familiar, or the shocking, or the most glamorous surface of excitement. It is blind to color, shape, association, dream.

The eye becomes as functionless as an appendix, atrophies. "So what else is new?" Exposed to everything, it sees nothing.

The same fate overcomes the ear. The same, the nose, and taste, and touch. The primary sensibility is reserved for mathematics: quantity, size, utility. The secondary qualities—subjective, personal, to each his own—do not improve one's status, position, wealth, or power. Only one's humanity.

A dinner in Utica is identical to a dinner in Topeka. Close your eyes, land at an airport, be driven down identical expressways into identical downtown areas, and study identical menus for dishes identically prepared.

The impoverishment of the senses, and sensuous feelings, and imaginative discriminations leaves the artist without an audience. Money Americans have; in need, taste, and desire many are deprived.

The living rooms of so many million homes are mass-produced. In one, in all. Yes, tastes differ and styles are various. Even the air is different. Magazines have instructed interior decorators how to make their rooms "distinctive." And yet . . . and yet . . .

So few are touched by art. Made, I mean, out of the sweat and labor and imagination of those who live there. Things, rather, are "acquired." So very little has been "made," "crafted," conceived in acts of love for materials and their possibilities. An old dresser scraped and stained —not in a way respectful of its grain, for the sake of the dresser, but in a way designed to look "attractive," for the sake of the governing taste of visitors.

How important it is for the possessions of an insecure people to "look nice." Not to give offense. To have undergone modern processing.

Process. Process. Process. The ugliest word, about which there is a whole philosophy! The American God is like tomato soup.

How, then, to redeem a culture of mass production? Make fun of it. Playfulness.

Not exactly. For the secret hidden in the vast processes pouring forth the waxy wrappers for Wonder Bread is the secret of mathematics: heedlessness of tongue, and touch, and ear, and eye, solicitous only of quantity. The wonderful folks who bring us Wonder Bread also bring us body count. The disease endures through war and peace. Reason is victor, sensuousness lies dead.

The secret is horror, and loneliness, and desperation. Humans shriven of humanity.

Humanity does not reside in number but in kind. More humanity in the taste buds of the tongue than in all the cost sheets of all the corporations of the land.

May blood-red Reason die. And may we all, peacefully and soon, return to our senses.

Thirty-Eight

The March wind howls. A basket of air gusts against the window of my eyrie, high above the street. Will winter never cease?

The lights in neighbors' windows have gone out. Do only artists love the night? Other men commute: they rise at six. Solar plexus, *punch*.

The paper under my hand is white. What will fill it? Thoughts there, buried out of sight, will not arise. The subject I've set myself is "creativity." As I was driving on an errand late this afternoon feelings spoke to me: I had to say something about the struggle to create.

Perhaps because I was discouraged. What I had written earlier today did not seem right. Neither its substance nor its tone. Progress is so slow!

Ah well, I start again. And then again. Give it to the typist, and look at it tomorrow. Tomorrow and tomorrow.

Can it be that writing is a dodge? One day, will I regret the hours spent at my desk? Scribble, scribble, man. Scribble, scribble. And what will there be to show for it? A life lived. Lived? Can writing be a life?

The loneliness of art is long. A painter faces her canvas all alone. Suppose her work is not in tune with fads. No, not even in tune with feelings people like to face. What she likes to do, what is her way, terrifies.

Museums do not call or answer queries. Buyers do not buy. The galleries are cautious. It is no longer worthwhile to telephone: the two canvasses they agreed to keep last fall have not been sold. The drawings, yes, the clerk believes they're in the rack—no, not sold, she's pretty sure. Well, thanks.

It is a lonely life. Every day an act of courage. Wrestling with one's doubts.

And what is it worth? Another book? A painting to hang on someone's wall? Perhaps no one will ever look at it, ever really look.

The world will not be changed. Perhaps no single person will be changed. Plain it is: the world is not redeemed through art. Not even the geniuses believe that, or should.

The work of art is only half created by the artist. The perceiver must create the other half. Creation is a communal affair.

And perhaps the little birds that Plato saw divided into two, each seeking everywhere its mate—perhaps my half will find no mate. Ofter work goes into the vastness echolessness.

Is it deception, art? A lie we tell? A fictive blending of our fantasies and ·needs, with no response? Self-centered act, ending whence it sprang? A circle closed?

Creativity. It is a mystery. So much inside me dies, is twisted, turns barren, groans. Yet there is need to face that emptiness.

Always worried, too, that what results is poor. Always fearful of snatching back the curtain farther than one ought, revealing far too much. Writing is so intimate an act. A hostile or indifferent audience steps back from words, sees them naked on the page, rips aside protective artifice . . . finds this page dull, that pretentious, the other one too superficial, that too dense.

What shall I do?

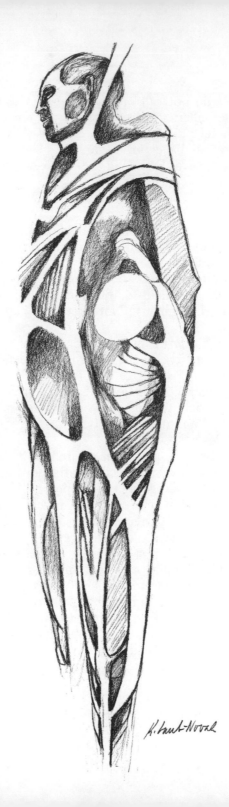

Lower my head, I know, continue on.

One does not work for an audience. Not quite. Perhaps for a mystic body, perhaps for an unseen horde or single soul. But never able to rely on that. One writes, in the end, for oneself. Writing is a personal act. Exorcism, some have said: casting out words that boil inside, a thousand swine of Gaza driven out, out, out and over the cliff.

It is, to be sure, like Genesis. The troubled waters roll. Without form, and void. And one must find it in oneself to enter the dark, not knowing what will come of it.

So many efforts stillborn. So many pages gone unread.

Like a painter with canvasses stacked wall-to-wall. No one can even see them. Lumber, fiber, pigment, vagrant images. Feelings long ago decayed.

The scent of death is never far away.

And yet there is a silent exultation. Out of night, sometimes, the day begins to break. Into humors and fog, clean air and light occasionally cut. The coruscating joy of it! A sentence placed exactly. A page which might endure. Brushwork delicate and bold, conception realized.

At night, sometimes, exhausted, one goes to bed with silent-singing heart. Poor Shakespeare, poor Michelangelo!

Then one regards one's work by light of day. Old, familiar sickness seeps into the lower regions of the stomach, rises, chokes . . . One must begin again to wrestle with oneself. Against despair. Against the longing to be quit of it.

Oh God, deliver me. Deliver me from torment! Don't you see!

One learns a certain sympathy for the gods of the creation myths. Was it ever a matter of a word, a thought, a simple clicking of the fingers: There, like that? "Let there be light!"

Was not the crucifixion, though coming late, endured by gods expectantly? Was there not agony at night before creative day?

Whatever it was for gods, for men creation has a price.

Thirty-Nine

God reveals himself as night. Dark fire, night flame. I am air.

The way is not through joy, tranquility, love, community . . . not through ecstasy, bravery, witness, affirmation . . . not through celebrating life, or trust, or human goodness . . . Mainly, it is night . . . and empty air.

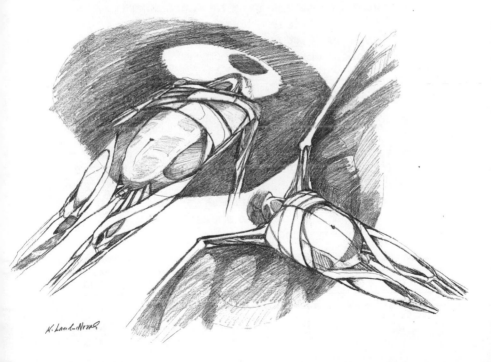

Between this night and atheism not a single hair . . .

The emptiness of atheism . . . and the emptiness of God—coincide. The humanist seems as right in his interpretation as anyone . . .

If there were not a certain silence in my heart, a certain quiet place, a certain perception that God does not grant favors—offers no refuge—to those who recognize him, I would probably long since have ceased to love him.

It is not a choice, exactly. Limpidity.

I do not "believe" in God. There is translucence in my heart. Less metaphorically: Somehow I have known that every act of creativity, honesty, freedom, courage, light is participant in him. These give me ecstasy. Each seems improbable.

To act in such ways is to be.

To be is to be dwelled in by another.

Some students believe in progress, reason, human goodness. I look at them as if they are insane.

Do they live in some other world?

Everywhere I see ego, lies, pretenses, deviousness . . . deception so deep the line between conscious and unconscious, willful and involuntary, scarcely matters . . . so sad we are . . . Not least, the students, not least professors! Pledged to truth, how tormented in their secret egos . . . how susceptible to status, flattery, illusion . . . Vomitous . . .

Light finds purchase in poor air but feebly . . .

If a single human being spoke nothing but the truth, reality could not support him . . . he would be deemed an idiot, destroyed . . . To speak (see and feel) nothing but the truth is to condemn oneself to death.

The abyss is unendurable . . .

. . . And every act of honesty miraculous.

Honesty did not have to enter into history (that void), did not have to come to be . . . it was created, is, resists, stands out (*ex-sistere*) against the nothingness . . . echoes the first creative act of God: "Let there be Light!" . . . refracts down shadowy corridors, in rooms of sheerest pitch . . .

The father of lies predominates . . . rules even children's lives . . . so phoney children are, and fake, manipulative, piercing keen . . . so close, however, to creative birth that juices of that miracle anoint their brows . . .

Forty

Holy Week. I try to tell the children the story of Jesus.
It is so difficult! Why was there blood upon the door at
Passover? Why did the angel kill the firstborn sons?
How did he do it? (Firstborn son is clearly troubled.)

What is an angel, a him or she?

Daddy, do *we* have ghosts? In our bodies, too?

No, no, children, that isn't what I meant!

Daddy, how did he rise again? Where did he go? How
come?

Who is God?

Some of the simpler things I cannot bring myself to
say. My stomach not at peace. What can it mean to
them? What can I find it in myself to say?

God makes things grow, and living things alive . . .

Did he make the fishes what suddenly grew legs
like us?

. . . It's like when you try to think, and you suddenly
have a thought. He helps you understand.

He doesn't help me to think. Sometimes I can't even
think of numbers and he doesn't help.

Daddy, did he make seeds?

Well, he made the trees that make their seeds.

He put all the food in the grocery store, didn't he?

He made things grow, and men gathered them and
brought them to the store.

Is Jesus living now?
In you and me and everyone.
[Puzzlement.]
Well, he rose up again, right? He should be living then.
Daddy, will we rise up too?
She is too young to have the faintest idea what that would mean, but it is plain she knows I will approve.
Forever and forever.
Holy smokes! [He rolls his eyes.] And never die?
Eeeee! [He falls back upon the pillow. Clearly crazy.]
You didn't tell us how he died . . .
I was coming to that.
. . . Or about the thorns. How long were they? Did they have points?
Why did the policemen do that, Daddy?

*   *   *

What is it one is doing when one teaches them? How can one focus on the crucial things?
My children, listen. Expect the world to be evil. Don't be surprised when men are cruel. When you are trying to be honest and be brave, then God is living in you. When you are alone, you are still with everybody—all are one, even in the silence, even when you're desperate.
Try to share. Cooperate. Don't be afraid of anger or of hate, neither in yourselves nor in others.
Strive, and grow. You are meant to be as God. His life is in you now, trying to expand. Allow it to. You are free, you won't be forced, if you want God to shine through you, you must allow him to.
History is very bloody. Oppression happens every day. Don't be afraid to suffer. Don't be afraid to fail. Try to help all men be one. Don't give up working hard at things like that.
At night, in the heart of things, there is often failure.

Jesus died. All his best friends ran away. Failure doesn't hurt.

Children, listen to me. Never be afraid. You are brave and you are true. Even when you're bad, it doesn't mean you aren't still loved. You're loved because you're you. Give it, give it back to God: give you.

*   *   *

How, daddy, how?

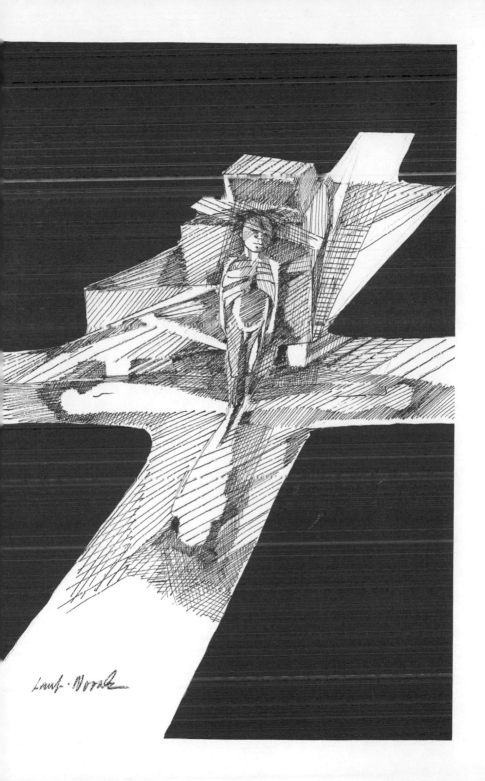

About the Author

Michael Novak, author of *The Experience of Nothingness* and other books, is associate professor of philosophy and religious studies at the State University of New York, Old Westbury. Karen Laub-Novak has exhibited paintings and prints in America and Europe, and won a competitive commission to excute a bronze statue of the winner of the Nobel Peace Prize, Norman E. Borlaug. The Novaks have two children, Richard and Tanya, with a third one racing this book to birth.